PAPER
folded·cut·sculpted

by Florence Temko

Illustrated by Virginia Davidson

COLLIER BOOKS
A Division of Macmillan Publishing Co., Inc.
NEW YORK

COLLIER MACMILLAN PUBLISHERS
LONDON

Macmillan Publishing Co., Inc.
866 Third Avenue, New York, N.Y. 10022
Collier-Macmillan Canada Ltd.

Library of Congress Catalog Card Number: 73–2125

First Collier Books Edition 1974

Paper: Folded, Cut, Sculpted
is also published in a hardcover edition by
Macmillan Publishing Co., Inc.

Art direction and design by Joan Stoliar
Design associate Virginia Davidson

Printed in the United States of America

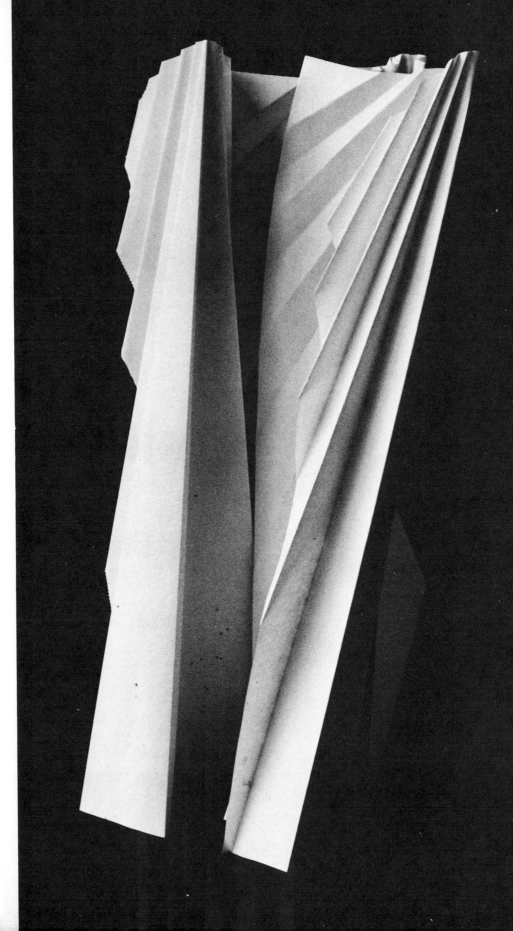

To
Lillian Oppenheimer—
an inspiration

Chinese Paper cut-outs,
actual size

ACKNOWLEDGMENTS

My knowledge of paper craft has been increased immeasurably over the years through contact with artists working in the same medium. I recall with special pleasure the meetings of the Origami Center in New York, presided over by Lillian Oppenheimer. Her warm and loving personality sparked my interest in paper craft.

Robert Harbin of England and Samuel Randlett of the United States, through their own books, have helped me clarify ideas on the difficult task of presenting instructions.

There are many other people who have shared their time and ideas with me. Regretfully it is impossible to mention them individually, but I thank my friends all over the world.

I believe my husband, Henry Petzal, is very happy to see the book in print for more than the usual reasons: he no longer has to read and reread the manuscript.

And if it had not been for Constance Schrader, my editor, who guided the book through several precarious adventures, you and I would not be meeting here.

CONTENTS

Armillary Spheres by Seymour Robins,
outstanding American designer of
packaging and graphics, whose work
is in major museums.

PAPER · FOLDED ORIGAMI

PAPER · CUT KIRIGAMI

PAPER · SCULPTED

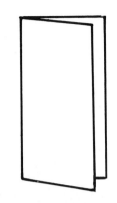 

SYMBOL FOR ORIGAMI
(PAPER FOLDED)

SYMBOL FOR KIRIGAMI
(PAPER CUT)

SYMBOL FOR SCULPTURE
(PAPER SCULPTED)

ARRANGEMENT OF THE BOOK

The book begins with a General Introduction and is then divided into three sections:

1 Paper Folded (origami), using paper only, without the aid of any tools.

2 Paper Cut (kirigami), using paper with the help of scissors or knife.

3 Paper Sculpted, three-dimensional designs fastened with glue, staples or other means.

For easy reference, each section is keyed by a symbol in a triangle in the top right-hand corner:

O for origami.

K for kirigami.

S for sculpture.

Each section is divided into two subsections:

Background and Procedures.

The Background section includes history, legend and other information of general interest.

This is followed by the Procedures which teach paper craft techniques in a systematic manner.

New procedures are indicated in the top right-hand corner. This helps you find the page where a particular technique is introduced. Pages without a label give instructions for additional practice models to reinforce previous procedures.

The final section of the book, the Appendix, offers practical information and is based on the questions I am asked most frequently about paper craft.

A NOTE ABOUT THE MEASUREMENTS. All measurements are given in inches followed by numbers in parentheses which repeat the measurements in centimeters. In order to avoid fractions, these measurements may not always correspond.

GENERAL INTRODUCTION

This book is intended for anyone with the desire to find out how paper can be made into decorative and useful things, and can be used as a craft course, a reference book or just read for pleasure. It is broadly grouped into folding, cutting and sculpture, the three methods of paper construction. Papier-mâché and découpage are not included, as they rely on other materials for stability. You will find a summary of established techniques: realistic, abstract, geometric and fanciful. You will also find historical information and anecdotes about people interested in the art.

We take for granted that paper will hold our groceries, carry print for newspapers or books and will serve hundreds of other purposes, but it is not usually recognized that it can be a craft medium. In the craft explosion that is taking place all around us, people are rediscovering the pleasure of making things with their hands and paper is a familiar material that can satisfy this urge for self-expression. The fact that it is colorful, flexible and widely available makes it an excellent material for experimentation by beginners; and yet a piece of paper offers plenty of challenge to the most advanced craftsman.

My interest began with origami which, in its purest form, does not permit any cutting or pasting. After a few years paper cutting appealed to me and I discovered that this was easier, yet equally fascinating and fulfilling. Later I recognized paper sculpture as a means of combining folding and cutting effectively.

Paper: Folded, Cut, Sculpted brings together my experience of working with paper, conducting many classes and lectures, and meeting with paper craft artists all over the world. Over a period of time I developed a new method of teaching paper craft, whereby it is possible for a beginner to make a complete design within minutes and, with one added step, another complete design. At any point you can produce your own variations and create your own original *objets d'art* or objects of use. In this book I have tried to convey the joy I felt the first time I made a paper puppet and the feeling of excitement that continues over the years. It is such fun to fold a toy for a child and see his face light up as he watches an ordinary piece of paper change into a bird that flaps its wings. Yet a challenging design that requires hours or days of work can give me a completely different kind of satisfaction. I hope this book will be a self-service store for you and that you will enjoy it.

Paper Cutting, by Hans
Christian Andersen, famous
Danish author of fairy tales.
Courtesy H.C. Andersens
Hus, Odense.

FAMOUS PEOPLE

In view of the versatility of paper, it is not surprising that many famous people have succumbed to its fascination as a hobby. Leonardo da Vinci (1452–1519), was the first to fold a paper airplane. Lewis Carroll (1832–1898), author of *Alice in Wonderland* and an outstanding mathematician, delighted in the art of paper folding, as did the English poet Percy Bysshe Shelley (1792–1822). Hans Christian Andersen (1805–1875), whose fairy tales have enchanted millions of children, illustrated some of his stories with fanciful paper cuts which are exhibited in his hometown of Odense in Denmark.

A delightful story is told about Leo Tolstoy (1828–1910), author of *War and Peace* and *Anna Karenina.* One day he was traveling on a tram with a friend. He made the ticket into an elaborate cockerel, which fluttered its wings when he pulled the tail (see flapping bird, page 83). Tolstoy presented it smilingly to the ticket collector who, in bureaucratic fashion, unfolded it, checked the number, and tore it up.

The famous American magician Houdini (1874–1926) was best known as an escape artist but his repertoire included some paper magic. One of his tricks was to transform a piece of paper into a flapping bird. He actually prefolded the paper, but his quick action and the stage lighting rendered the creases invisible.

PAPER CRAFTS IN THE PAST

First let us delve into the origins of paper. Curiously there is one family that holds a continuous record of production: the wasp, which builds its nest from wood pulp. Wood pulp is still the main substance of commercially produced paper, although all kinds of leaves and rags can be used.

The story of paper began 5,000 years ago with the Egyptians who used papyrus, a reed which grows in the Nile Delta. Then, about 100 A.D., the Chinese invented the present method of paper making. Mulberry leaves were part of the pulp and this is still an ingredient in Japanese handmade papers. In about the fifteenth century, from China, paper reached Europe via Persia and Arabia.

The main purpose of paper was to convey written messages, but even at an early date paper was folded in specific ways to convey symbolic messages, particularly in the Orient. Later on, during the eighteenth century, when both scissors and paper became cheaper as a result of the invention of machinery, the vogue for paper crafts started in Europe and America. Most popular was silhouette portrait cutting, described on page 117. Other designs were made by paper pricking, whereby the paper is painstakingly pierced with needles to give a perforated effect. A Mrs. Delaney created a collection of beautiful lifelike flowers in paper mosaics almost 300 years ago; this curiosity is now in the British Museum in London. In Germany baptismal certificates and other family documents were folded and decorated in artistic ways and kept in the family Bible (see illustration).

A magician's trick that has delighted audiences for a long time and is still in use today is the troublewit, a large piece of strong pleated paper that can be turned into a chair, a parasol, a lantern and many other things with just the flick of the wrist.

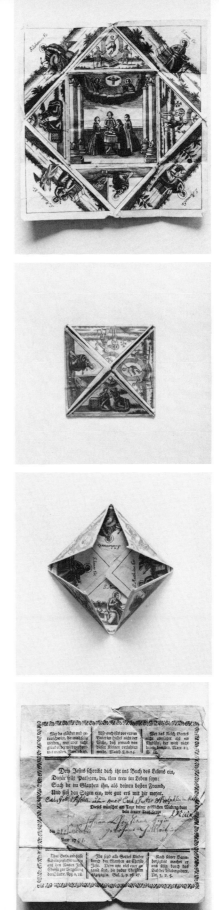

German Baptismal
Certificate,
18th century

Chinese Burial Robe
Author's Collection, Photograph:
Courtesy, The Museum of
Contemporary Crafts, New York.

Gold and Red Prayer Money

chinese burial papers

Chinese Burial Papers may be considered a form of paper sculpture with roots far back in history.

It is well known that gifts were buried in the tombs in the Egyptian pyramids to accompany the dead to the afterworld. A similar custom existed in China. Between the sixth and ninth centuries clay figures of horses, dancers and musicians were placed in graves as religious symbols. They have been unearthed in good condition and are now in such great demand that they have been counterfeited. In time the clay figures were replaced by paper replicas of slaves, furniture, robes, musical instruments, trunks, boats, toys, anything that would make life agreeable in the hereafter.

These unusual artifacts are mentioned in various books about China and paper craft, but no one to whom I spoke in the United States had actually seen them. When I had the opportunity to travel in the Orient I succeeded in locating a shop in Singapore which was filled from floor to ceiling with the greatest variety of burial papers, some quite costly, others priced in pennies. Elaborate gowns for men and women, horses, baby shoes, anything imaginable was imitated in paper and decorated with watercolor paint and paper cut-outs. Bundles of imitation money made of a rough quality paper with a central square of fine gold paint were intended to appease evil spirits. Despite their funereal purpose, the objects were absolutely delightful and highly colorful.

Relatives of recently deceased persons bought these paper objects before visiting the Buddhist temple across the street. After burning incense and offering prayers they burned them in a tremendous ten-foot-high sacred urn as a religious offering to their ancestors.

This ritual was observed in China until the end of the last century. To a small extent it still exists in Singapore and Hong Kong, two cities with large Chinese populations, but even there the custom is dying out, as it is considered superstitious by modern people.

Three-dimensional collapsible
store decoration; Coca-Cola
Company

Henri Matisse, *Nuit de Noel.*
1952. Maquette for stained glass
window commissioned by Life,
1952. Gouache on paper, cut and
pasted, 10'7" x 53½". (Collection,
The Museum of Modern Art,
New York; Gift of Time Inc.)

20

MODERN PAPER CONSTRUCTION

In the twentieth century professional painters and artists have followed in the footsteps of Pablo Picasso (1881–1973), using paper as an art medium in collage and assemblage (three-dimensional collage). The French painter Henri Matisse (1869–1954), brought paper cutting to its highest artistic point. He was fascinated by color and made his most forceful statement in pure abstract form by cutting enormous, brightly colored sheets of paper into shapes which he rearranged until he was satisfied. He felt that this method offered him greater flexibility than paint.

The most dramatic paper designs are now created by anonymous artists in industry. Through research they discovered the properties peculiar to paper and developed new packaging, decorations, toys, clothing and furniture which make our lives more convenient and visually attractive. These functional objects are often very beautiful.

PHILOSOPHY

One of the reasons that paper is not usually considered an art or craft medium may be its impermanent nature. People like to create something lasting and paper denies them this satisfaction.

Although many useful items are described in this book, the essential charm of paper is that a momentary creation can give pleasure to you and others. If you fold a paper animal and crush it, it will have existed. A paper bird can give joy just as the flowers of spring, although we know they will fade. The Japanese people make long trips to admire cherry trees in bloom. Because the blossoms remain for such a short time they are a symbolic reminder of the impermanence of life. This transitory feeling is deeply rooted in Zen Buddhism.

Yet it is not only Far Eastern philosophy that is stirring interest in paper arts. If, as Alvin Toffler asserts in his book *Future Shock,* we are living in a throw-away society, then paper is the ideal art medium. It invites experimentation and says to young and old alike: "Come and try this; experience the creative feeling." There is a challenge in turning a basic material into something unique which could not be made by anyone else. The concentration required permits us to take time out from thinking about everyday cares and feel relaxed. Through this involvement our hands and eyes gain experience which enriches our lives.

HOW TO USE THE PAPER CRAFT DESIGNS

A few suggestions on how to make use of paper constructions will be found throughout the book, but they have been kept to a minimum so that they do not obscure the basic techniques. Of course much of the fun is in making decorations and toys and as you go along, you will probably think of many applications yourself. If you plan to make something specific—a greeting card, Christmas decorations—you can get many ideas by looking critically at each model in the book to see whether it could be adapted to your purpose. Here is a collection of ideas:

Banners   Roll top edge of a large piece of paper over a dowel.

Bas-relief pictures and plaques   Use paper sculpture procedures.

Book covers   Use brown wrapping paper and decorate it.

Border designs   Repeat patterns; cut shapes from pleated paper, use leftover paper scraps.

Bulletin boards   Most of the illustrated techniques can be used.

Cake decorations   Attach origami figures to thin sticks or ice cream sticks, merry-go-round fashion.

Calendars   Create a variation on a theme for each month of the year.

Chains and garlands   How about stretch paper? Strands of flowers made from newspaper, with colored centers.

Christmas ornaments   Almost any shape can be a Christmas ornament when made from foil-backed giftwrap paper. Some of the beginning steps of origami models can be made in varying sizes and colors.

Collage   Combine magazine illustrations with three-dimensional paper designs. Make a patchwork pattern from a variety of textured papers.

Community projects   Boy and Girl Scout troops and other youth organizations can perform a service to the community by making holiday and other favors for sick

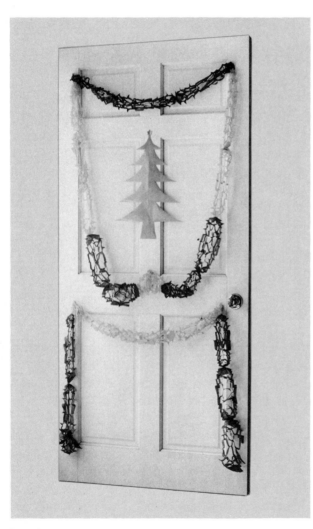

Door Decoration (See pages 127 and 133 for techniques.)

children in the hospital, folded valentines, turkey cut-outs, birthday gifts.

Containers   Make fantasy animals from cans, cartons and plastic bottles.

Embroidery patterns   Polish and Chinese cut-outs.

Fans   Pleated fans can be attached to gift packages or to Christmas trees.

Flags   Look at international flags for design ideas.

Gifts   A pack of origami paper or a few sheets of gift-wrap paper can provide hours of entertainment.

Giftwrapping decorations   Make giant flowers; paste Mexican cut-outs onto a contrasting color background; make a gift card to match the wrapping paper; for sending through the mails, attach pop-up decorations.

Greeting cards   Decorate appropriately for the occasion.

Hats   Parties and children's parades.

Holiday decorations   Halloween, Valentine's Day, bon voyage parties.

Illustrations for reports   Decorative headings. Cut-out illustrations.

Invitations   Pop-up constructions.

Jewelry   Spray paper models with acrylic to harden them.

Kites   Experiment with different shapes.

Memo pads   Personalize the cover.

Metal sculpture patterns   Paper designs can be used as patterns for sheet metal sculpture.

Mobiles   Suspend origami figures from a wire clothes-hanger or a cardboard circle.

Packages   Odd-shaped packages can be wrapped in newspaper and then decorated.

Party favors   Nut cups, placecards, centerpieces, door prizes.

Placemats   Decorate them with cut-outs.

Pop-ups   Greeting cards, toys and surprise gifts.

Posters   Make them from cut-out designs or attach three-dimensional forms.

Report covers   Relate the design to the subject matter.

Room decorations   Bunch paper flowers to fill in empty spaces; make oversize animals. Auditoriums and large halls require large-scale decorations of giant tissue flowers, posters or chains made from strong paper.

Room dividers   Glue flat or folded shapes onto screens; use road maps.

Sculptures and stabiles   Add importance by placing them on pedestals which can be made from covered boxes.

Stationery   Make designs relating to your hobby, profession, pets; make border designs.

Stencils   Cut-outs made from strong paper can be painted over to leave a pattern that can be repeated. Paper tiles can be made this way.

Table decorations   Co-ordinate the colors of the centerpieces, nut cups and napkin folds with the colors of the tablecloth and room decor.

Telephone book covers Paste on a collage of paper cutouts.

Toys   Make action toys as gifts; design puzzles.

Wall pictures   Group several together.

Wax paper laminates   Place a paper cut-out between two layers of wax paper. Press with a warm iron.

Windows   Frame a window with paper designs instead of curtains; paste cut-outs on window panes; appliqué cut-outs to window shades.

Combining paper with other materials   The directions given in the book show paper used in its purest form, but you can add ribbons, glitter, buttons, shells, found objects, colored cellophane tape, felt pen lines, any common or uncommon item you like.

Sources for further ideas   Magazine illustrations, advertisements, historical costumes, books on other crafts. Books about magic sometimes include paper tricks.

PAPER

FOLDED ORIGAMI

fold here

fold here

ORIGAMI
CONTENTS

PAPER · FOLDED ORIGAMI

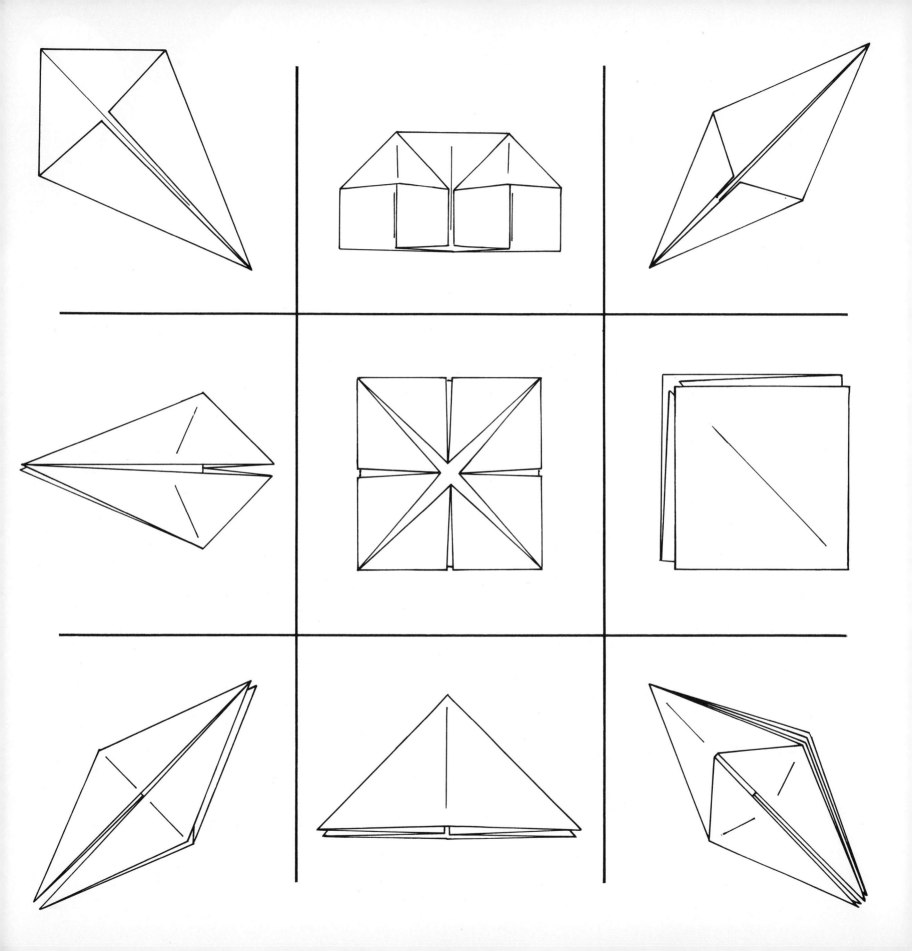

INTRODUCTION

Origami is a Japanese word that is now accepted all over the world for the art of paper folding. In translation *ori* means folding and *gami* means paper. It describes the art of folding a piece of paper into a figure, decoration or action toy without cutting or pasting. Most people come across paper folding at an early age when someone makes a hat from a newspaper and then turns it into a boat, but it is not generally realized that this is an elementary form of one of the oldest paper crafts. There are countless simple figures that can be mastered in minutes by a beginner, but a more sophisticated model may have as many as 250 folds. This means that a large square of paper, say 30″ (75 cm), may be folded back and forth according to an intricate design until it is reduced to about 8″ (20 cm) and is several layers thick in spots.

The Origami Procedures section in the book shows established techniques for making many easy folded models, as well as some of intermediate complexity and a few advanced designs. The advanced models are not all grouped at the end, but are placed where they develop naturally.

The word "base" is used in the following sense: some sequences of folds are constantly used as the beginning for many different models. For convenience these sequences are called bases.

A frequent comment about books on paper folding is that the instructions are too difficult to follow. It *is* necessary to follow every word and diagram and that requires patience for the more complicated models. It also sometimes happens that a book translated from the Japanese presupposes a certain familiarity with origami. The directions in this book have been tested by friends and neighbors, who made the models without my assistance, to make sure they are as clear as possible.

Origami can be a challenging craft but it is also entertaining. It is fascinating to watch the magic of a piece of paper being turned into an animal or toy. I usually carry some paper squares with me, but even when I do not have any, there always seems to be some sort of paper available when the occasion for paper folding presents itself. Magazine pages, paper napkins or placemats, stationery or advertisements can be put to work and, if nothing else can be found, a money bill is always an added attraction. The only drawback is that giving away samples can become expensive! I have made origami for a child in a doctor's waiting room, for businessmen on long plane journeys, newspaper hats against a broiling sun and on innumerable other occasions; sometimes it turned a few dull hours into an impromptu party. Origami is an icebreaker and anyone with a repertoire of only two or three simple objects can quickly make friends. Whether you become a paper folding aficionado or not, you can have a lot of fun with origami and it will help you communicate with other people wherever you may be.

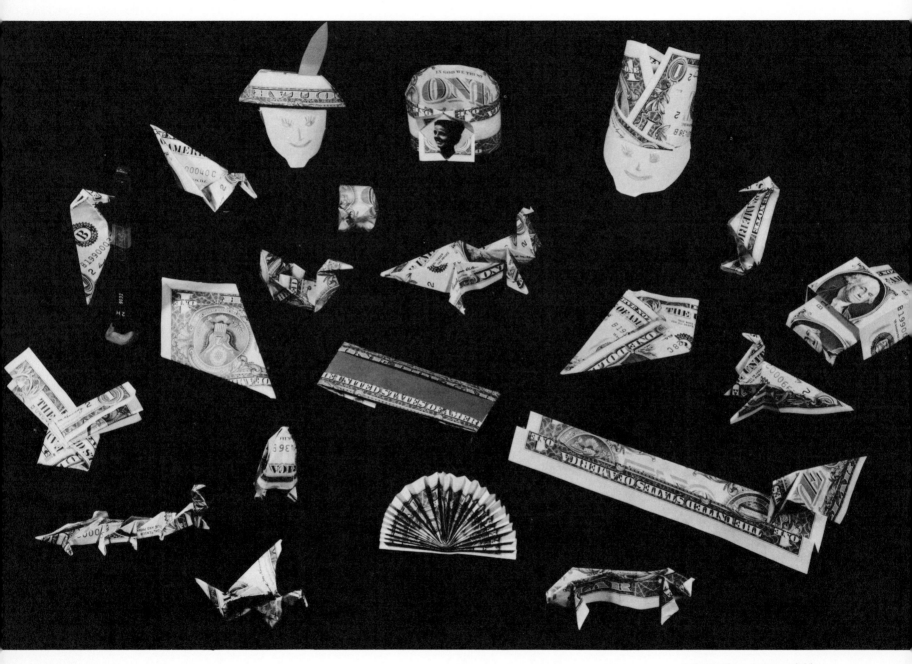

A Collection of money folds

the rules of paper folding

The rules of paper folding according to the strictest Japanese tradition are:

1 The paper must not be cut or glued in any way.

2 A fold once made must not be unmade, thus the model becomes smaller and smaller.

3 A three-dimensional figure should be capable of being collapsed flat.

Some practitioners adhere strictly to these rules, but others interpret them more liberally and may make a small cut when that will greatly enhance the character of the model. An example is the shrimp on page 73.

background

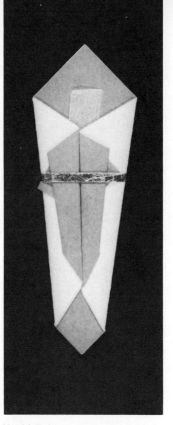

Noshi Fold, customarily
attached to gifts in Japan.

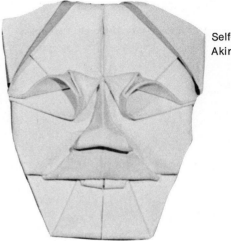

Self-Portrait by
Akira Yoshisawa.

Three Mice, by Japanese Master
of origami, Akira Yoshisawa,
from an exhibit at the Cooper
Union Museum, New York.

china

Paper was reputedly invented in China by Tsai Lun in 105 A.D. and it is generally believed that paper folding originated in China as part of the custom of burying paper articles with the dead. In more recent times paper folding has become the happy activity of children.

japan

Most people associate the art of paper folding with Japan and it is true that it is the only country where it is an integral part of the culture, to be found in the home and in centuries-old ceremonies and festivals. The earliest reference to paper folding is in an eleventh-century novel about court life. It is mentioned that a lady, trying to write a love poem, impatiently folds a piece of paper into a house.

The first book showing how to make animals appeared at the end of the eighteenth century, and was followed by a period when the education of a young lady included origami, along with the tea ceremony and flower arranging.

An ancient practice still continuing today is the custom of attaching *noshi* folds to all gifts. *Noshi* are small paper squares, red on one side and white on the other, folded in prescribed patterns according to elaborate rules of etiquette. They always express wishes for good fortune but the folding patterns vary with the gift. For example, a gift of candy requires a different pleating pattern than a basket of fruit. As formality declined over the years, *noshi* became simplified; today only a few patterns are used. Ready folded *noshi* are provided in Japanese stores, whenever a purchase is intended as a gift, or the donor can make his own. *Noshi* folds are closely related to other types of ceremonial folds used at specific festivals and celebrations. For weddings, gold and silver paper is folded into butterflies as symbols for a happy marriage.

The best known origami figure is the classic crane, a favorite theme throughout Japanese art. It is symbolic of good fortune and longevity since, according to folklore, the crane lives for 1,000 years. It is estimated that seventy percent of the Japanese people are familiar with the folding procedure. As far back as 1799 "The Secret of Making One Thousand Cranes" was published. This intricate design shows how to fold 1,000 birds from a single sheet of paper by making strategically placed incisions, without cutting it apart. Each bird is folded from a square of paper

which is partially attached to other squares. Traditionally 1,000 cranes, usually folded from separate pieces of paper, will assure the health of a sick person. In recent years the crane has become the symbol of peace, and children from all over the world send folded cranes to be placed at the Hiroshima Peace Shrine for ceremonies which take place on the anniversary of the dropping of the first atomic bomb.

Most Japanese are familiar with origami and probably know how to make a few simple things which they learned in elementary school or at home, but I do not wish to give the impression that it is an all-consuming passion. Small children are taught traditional origami by their mothers and grandmothers, and designs are handed down through the generations in much the same way as are cooking recipes all over the world. It is not unusual for three- and four-year-old children to be able to fold boats and kimonos. They may receive origami paper as a small gift just as Western children receive coloring books.

Since about 1950 origami has been revitalized as an adult art form. There are several groups and clubs devoted to origami and their work is featured in newspapers, magazines and art exhibitions.

The outstanding master artist in Japan is Akira Yoshisawa, whose animal creations not only look real, but show their essential spirit. Even without an awareness of the underlying limiting rules of origami, one knows that these are great works of art. When I visited Tokyo, Yoshisawa received me in his home and, as a special honor, showed me his work. It seemed that the eight-legged paper cicada would jump right off the table. It took Yoshisawa twenty-three years and hundreds of experimental models to perfect this lifelike insect. Yoshisawa's life is dedicated to origami and he derives mystical satisfaction from his realistic and fantasy creations. Lately he has fashioned sculptured portraits of himself and famous people, an incredibly difficult task considering that they are achieved without any cutting. Yoshisawa devised the international system of written symbols used in this and other books and is the president of the International Origami Friendship Society.

Dokoutei Nakano is a younger origamist who shows promise. After only a few years he has produced some exciting models of great complexity. One of his innovations is to start with pieces of paper of unusual shapes, perhaps a half-star, which offer more flexibility.

Deer, by Fred Rohm, American.

Hat, by Robert Harbin, British

united states

In the United States interest in paper folding began in the mid-1950's. Early recognition was given by the Cooper Union Museum in New York, where an exhibition, "Plane Geometry and Fancy Figures," was staged in 1959. This exhibition was greatly aided by Lillian Oppenheimer, the director of the Origami Center in New York and a vital force in the world of paper folding. Her efforts have brought about much of the interest in origami as a hobby. She maintains the largest record of origami models and paper folders' names and addresses all over the world, which enables paper folders to keep in touch with one another. Whenever they meet there is a charged excitement in the air as they exchange new folds, making the hours pass like minutes.

The influence of origami is spreading in many areas and can be recognized in advertising and greeting cards. Many schools relate art and mathematics activities to paper folding and it has been accepted as beneficial in therapeutic work.

A few important American artists have emerged, among them Fred Rohm and Neal Elias, both of whom produce work of great beauty and originality. They have the rare ability to solve difficult technical tasks and they have actually created new concepts in paper folding. One of their innovations is to make designs from a double square (a rectangle in the proportion of 2 to 1) rather than the traditional square.

england

In England paper folding has been popularized by Robert Harbin, the president of the British Origami Society, who wrote *Paper Magic* in 1956, the first comprehensive introduction to paper folding with clear instructions intended for the English-speaking public. In 1970 he began a weekly ten-minute television program which persuaded millions of people to try their hand at paper folding.

germany

Kindergarten education and the Bauhaus art school are two movements of German origin which exerted widespread influence. Both employed paper folding as an educational tool.

Friedrich Froebel (1782–1852), founder of the kindergarten, introduced paper folding and cutting into the curriculum. Teachers studying his methods made scrapbooks of different folded and woven designs to encourage freedom of expression.

In the 1920's the Bauhaus revolutionized art education. Until that time wood, linen and other materials were destined for specific decorative or functional purposes. The Bauhaus handicrafts workshops encouraged students to inquire, without a set goal in mind, into the basic properties of the materials, such as their flexibility, strength and shape retention. Paper was one of the materials chosen since students had fewer preconceptions about what could be done with it. By experimenting they heightened their awareness and gave play to their imagination. The aim was to apply the newly gained insights to architecture and interior design, by combining machine methods and free artistic expression. The Bauhaus is the most important influence on modern paper construction and is largely responsible for the recognition of paper as a craft medium.

spain and argentina

In Spain and Argentina, paper folding is a method for teaching co-ordination between the mind and the hand. In Spain this interest was stimulated by Miguel de Unamuno (1864–1936), who was able to spread his joy in paper folding because of his fame as a novelist and philosopher. One of the foremost paper folders, Ligia Montoya (died 1967), lived in Argentina and was known for her delicate flowers and animals.

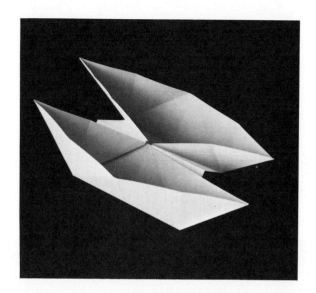

Froebel type fold (Multiform Base)

Flower, by Ligia Montoya, Argentinian.

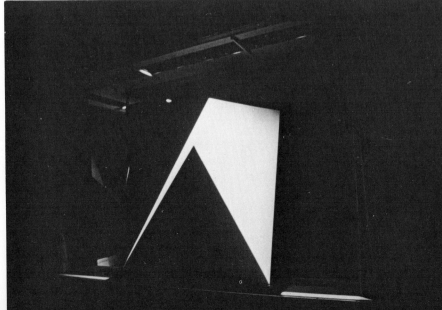

origami and mathematics

Many scientists and engineers are dedicated paper folders, which is probably because of the close relationship between origami and mathematics. I am very interested in this aspect of paper folding and have discussed it with several mathematicians and scientists. In spite of the obvious geometric patterns which are revealed when any model is unfolded, only a few isolated facts emerged:

It is possible to state the degrees of angles and the lengths of folded lines.

Some geometric processes can be executed easily by paper folding. For example, folding a corner in half is dividing a ninety-degree angle into two forty-five-degree angles.

Pleating paper creates parallel lines.

The IBM World Trade Corporation programmed their System 360 Model 91 computer to print out origami configurations. Folds were to be made in numerical order with a minus sign indicating a fold toward you (called a Valley Fold by paper folders and shown as a dotted line) and the absence of a sign indicating a fold away from you (a Mountain Fold shown as a line of dashes). The computer printed out about 100 configurations in less than a minute. According to the programmers, about ten percent of them were good. Subsequently they had to be folded by hand into three-dimensional form. The computer-generated origami designs were very simple and abstract, and in no way approached man-generated origami!

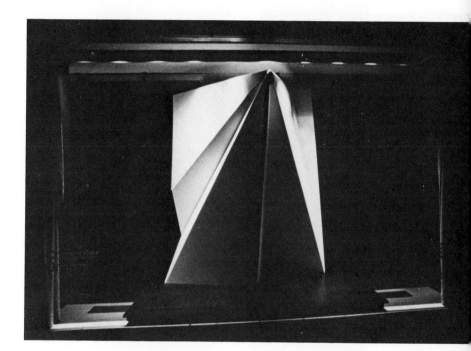

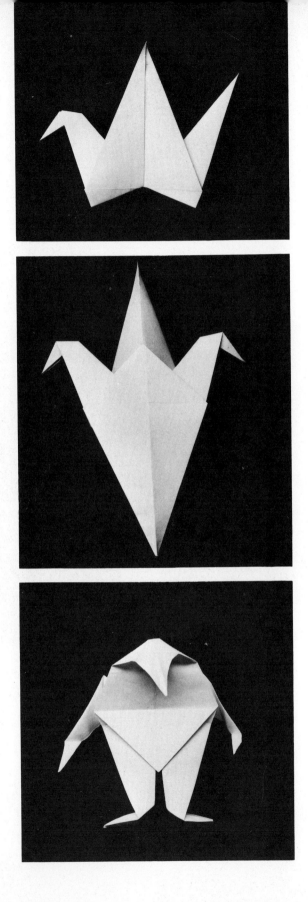

how to create new origami models

A question I am often asked is "Do you create your own origami patterns?" The answer is definitely "yes." I find it most challenging when I am requested to make something for a specific purpose. Once the theme for a church supper was "Around the World." A special committee was preparing paper folded decorations and particularly wanted a pineapple as the symbol for Hawaii. I did not know how to make an origami pineapple, so I adapted the ball on page 88.

When I am working on a model, a dog for example, I may see possibilities for making another four-legged animal, perhaps a horse. I will then try to bring out the characteristics of this animal, by changing Mountain Folds into Valleys, narrowing points, adding pleats or applying specific folding procedures, such as the Reverse Fold. When the model looks representative, I may continue to make small changes until I am completely satisfied that it is just right.

Creating origami is not as difficult as it may seem. Some of the models I have created have evolved almost by accident. It is difficult to describe just how it happens, but after you know how to make a few origami models you develop a feeling about what is possible and you "see" different figures. This is the first step toward invention. Children are less inhibited than adults and often see an animal, face or piece of furniture in a folded piece of paper. This enables them to create new designs without hesitation. Books and collections of origami models may help to inspire you and you may then share your interest with other paper folders for even greater stimulation and fun.

exhibits

Origami is suitable for exhibition at arts and craft shows. Models may be reinforced with wire, glue or plastic coating, and can be stuffed with cotton or facial tissue to maintain their three-dimensional shape. I have found that realistic figures, such as animals, as well as geometric decorations, are more readily accepted than abstracts. Purely abstract sculpture made according to the rules of origami has yet to be explored, but this is a natural artistic development that I find personally very challenging.

The concept of original art with regard to origami differs from that of other art media. The first painting or sculpture created by an artist is considered the original and reproductions made by another person are considered less important. Because of the perishable nature of the material used in origami, however, the artist-creator is always credited with the idea, regardless of the hands by which it is actually copied. For example, a butterfly conceived by Ligia Montoya will always be called Montoya's Butterfly, but there need not be a preserved original. Nevertheless, the indefinable quality of love and art often shines through a model made by the original creator. As in other fields, it sometimes happens that two or more people think of the same idea independently and both rightly claim the design as their own.

The angles of the folds and the colors of the foil paper used, are the essence of these Christmas tree decorations.

how to store and file origami models

Often when people have made a few different origami models they wish to keep them as a reminder of how they were made. At first they put them helter-skelter into a box, but soon a desire for greater orderliness is met with indecision about how to accomplish this. You may be interested in knowing how I store my extensive library of about 1,200 models, designed by myself and other artists.

When I began accumulating origami models, I placed each one into a separate envelope, together with several step folds. Step folds are separate pieces of paper which represent each folding operation necessary to make a complete origami and they make it very easy to reconstruct a model, particularly after a long period of time. I soon found, however, that I could not keep up with my files, because of the time involved in making the step folds. My present system is to file with or without step folds, but to include at least two completed figures, one to be kept in the final form and another for unfolding. I learned from bitter experience that the duplicate is a good idea since sometimes, like Humpty Dumpty, a model is difficult to put together again.

An improvement on paper envelopes is transparent plastic sandwich bags, in which the model is clearly visible. I include in the bag a 4″ x 7″ file card with the name of the originating artist, hints on how to fold and other pertinent information.

libraries

Artists from all over the world send details of their folds to the Origami Center in New York and to the British Origami Society in England, where they are catalogued and kept available for reference on request.

The New York collection will ultimately be housed at the Cooper-Hewitt Museum of the Smithsonian Institution, in New York. It is organized according to a system devised by Alice Grey, the editor of *The Origamian,* and is filed alphabetically in the following major categories:

Animals
Basic forms
Geometrics
Holidays
Legerdemain, including puzzles, riddles and magic.
Masks
Money folds
Objects (man-made models of)
Plants
Story series (progressive models)
Toys (for actual use by children)
Useful models (things practical for ordinary use)

size

Paper squares must be cut accurately to give good results. The kind of paper cutter sold in office stationery stores is a great help, although the paper can also be sized with scissors or an X-Acto knife.

Generally a good size of paper to use is between 5″ [12 cm] and 8″ [20 cm] square, but you may also need other sizes. For large scale decorations, paper up to 4′ [120 cm] square may be required. Since it is difficult to find paper in this width, sections of paper can be cellophane-taped together, but the edges must not overlap. Such large decorations may have to be reinforced with wire or wooden dowels.

A pair of tweezers is helpful for making tiny models. I know of a Japanese man who can make a crane from a ¼″ [3 mm] square, but I do not know what tools he uses.

If the final dimensions of a design must be of a specific size, it can only be ensured by trial and error. There is no constant relationship between the size of the piece of paper you start with and the size of the end result. An 8″ [20 cm] square may result in a 4″ [10 cm] boat or a 2″ [5 cm] bird, depending on the folding involved.

materials

Any paper that holds a crease well is suitable for paper folding. Special Japanese origami paper in brilliant colors and ready-cut in squares is available, but stationery, typewriter paper or magazine pages are less expensive. Giftwrap paper offers the greatest variety of colors and patterns. Paper backed giftwrap foil is very showy and makes gorgeous Christmas decorations. The thin layer of aluminum bonded to the paper gives long life to any project. Kitchen foil, however, is not suitable and wallpaper and construction paper are generally too brittle.

An important part of a well-executed origami model lies in the selection of paper. A rich green paper immediately suggests a frog and a small floral pattern adds humor to a calico cat. I once made a snake from tan paper, but I later discovered a reptile print which added a great deal of drama. Whenever I see an interesting piece of paper, whether gift wrapping, an advertisement or gray kraft paper, I add it to my collection to use at the appropriate time, but even so I sometimes have to search for several weeks in the

stores for just the right pattern for a specific design.

One particular kind of paper that holds a special fascination is money! From the paper folder's point of view the quality of the paper is excellent and holds a crease well. An origami money-fold gift is doubly appreciated.

folding terms

This glossary includes, in alphabetical order, standard paper folding terms used in the Procedures section, which follows. Page numbers indicate where each can be found.

Japanese handmade papers

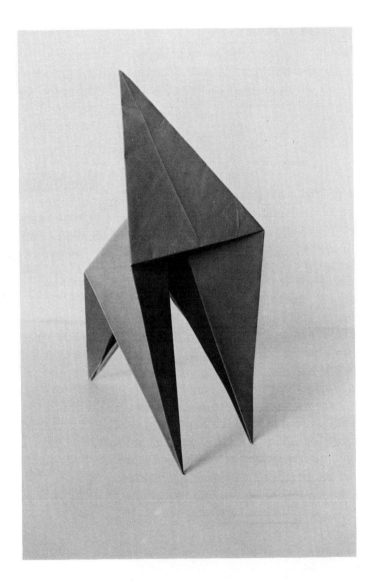

**how to
make a
square
from a
rectangle
of paper**

graphic symbols

VALLEY FOLD _____

MOUNTAIN FOLD ___ .. ___ .. ___ .. ___

TURN FIGURE OVER ⟲

FOLD AND UNFOLD ⟵

CREASE MADE PREVIOUSLY—thin incomplete line _____

CUT—heavy line and scissors _____ ✂

procedures

helpful folding hints

Work on a firm surface like a table top or a book.

Familiarize yourself thoroughly with the six graphic symbols.

Always make sharp, accurate creases.

Fold slowly.

Look ahead to the next drawing to see the step completed.

MOST IMPORTANT: Follow instructions carefully. Diagrams and written instructions are of equal importance. They are designed to complement each other. Reading the instructions out loud is helpful.

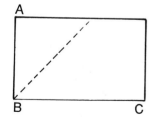

1. Fold edge A–B to lie along edge B–C.

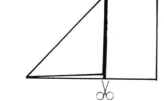

2. Cut off as shown.

3. Here is your square.

MOST ORIGAMI MODELS ARE MADE FROM SQUARES

45

Valley Fold and Mountain Fold are words used all the time by paper folders, people who enjoy making things out of paper without using scissors and glue, only adding their imagination to see what artistic things they can make.

mountain fold

Whenever the paper is
to be folded like this,
you will see
a line like this:_____.._____.._____.._____

MOUNTAIN FOLD

VALLEY FOLD

valley fold

Whenever the paper is
to be folded like this,
you will see
a line like this: — — — — — — — — — — — —

TO MAKE A GREETING CARD

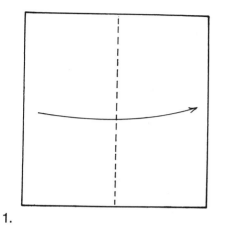

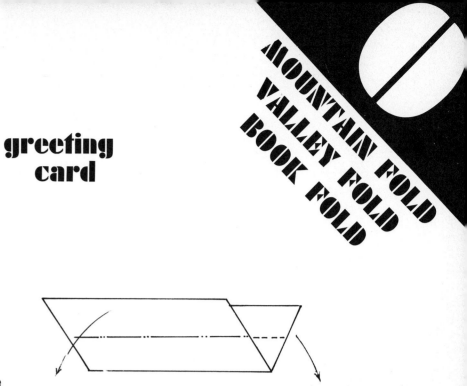

greeting card

1.
When holding a square piece of paper most people fold it in half like this.
This is a Book Fold.

2.
This simple step is the beginning of the art of paper folding. You have already made a Greeting Card.

3.
By folding down the two edges, one in front and one behind, you can make an Animal Feeding Trough.

animal feeding trough

When you look closely at the Trough you will see that the middle fold is like a valley and the two top folds are like mountains.

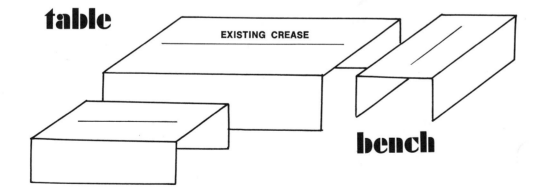

table

EXISTING CREASE

4.
The Trough can easily be made into a Table by leveling the center and standing it only on the two edges.

bench

Make a Table from a 6″ [15 cm] square of fairly stiff paper.
Fold two 4″ [10 cm] squares in the same way to make benches.

A thin incomplete line, as shown in the center of the table, means that there is a crease which was previously made in the paper.

47

TO MAKE A BOAT

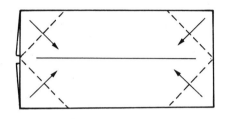

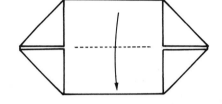

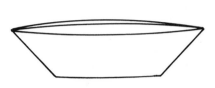

boat

1.
Flatten the Table so that smooth side is up. Fold four corners as shown by dotted lines and arrows.

2.
Fold in half lengthwise, hiding the four corners inside.

TO MAKE A PICTURE FRAME

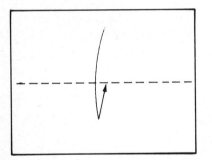

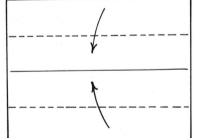

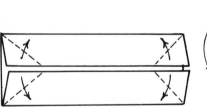

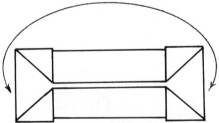

1.
If paper is colored on one side only, have colored side of paper up. Fold in half. Then unfold.

2.
Fold outer edges to center line.

3.
Fold all four corners (single layer of paper) from center outward, as shown by dotted lines and arrows.

4.
Roll paper and slide one end into the other. (To make this easier, first stretch paper over the edge of a table.)

8″ x 10″ [20 cm x 25 cm] is a good size of paper to frame a 3″ [8 cm] photograph.

A Picture Bracelet can be made by making the Picture Frame from a piece of paper 8″ x 2½″ [20 cm x 6 cm].

TO MAKE A LONGER BOAT

A rectangle placed in this direction makes a longer Boat.

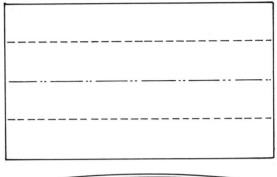

TO MAKE A HAT

Place a 22″ x 14″ [56 cm x 35 cm] rectangle of newspaper or gift wrap in this direction to make a hat that can be worn.

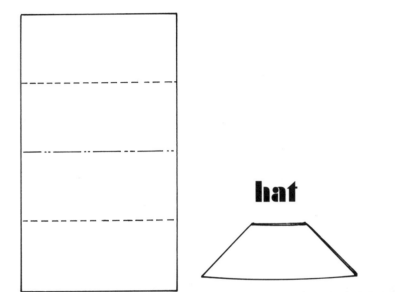

hat

picture frame

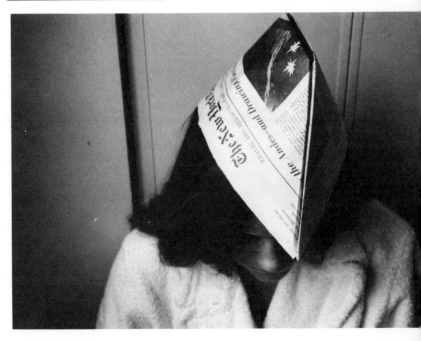

TO MAKE A FAN

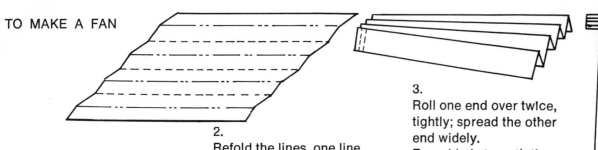

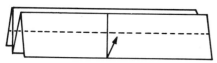

1.
The Trough on page 47 is the beginning of Accordion Pleating. From a square make the Trough. Fold in half lengthwise, then unfold the paper completely.

2.
Refold the lines, one line down (Valley Fold), the next one up (Mountain Fold), alternating this pattern in Accordion Pleats.

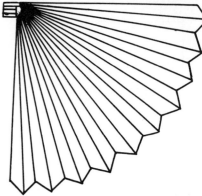

3.
Roll one end over twice, tightly; spread the other end widely.
For added strength the bottom of the fan may be stapled.

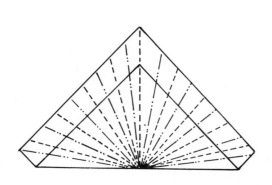

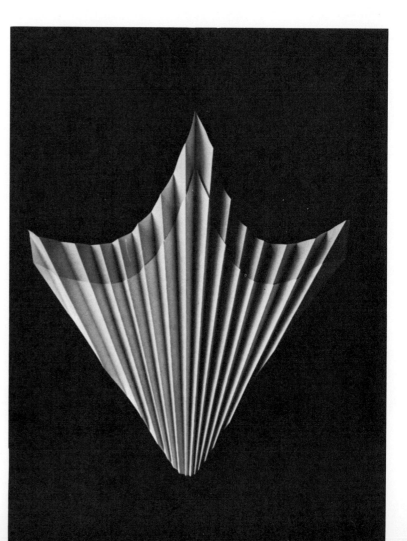

TO MAKE A SCREEN

Use a piece of paper in the proportion of 1 to 1½.
If you want the width of the Fan at the bottom to be
20″ [50 cm], use paper 20″ x 30″ [50 cm x 75 cm].

1.
Accordion pleat.

VARIATIONS:

Use longer piece of paper.
Use striped paper, either horizontally or vertically.
Add strip of contrasting paper on top edge, before
pleating.
Use flowered giftwrap.

2.
Secure center by stapling
or with cellophane tape.

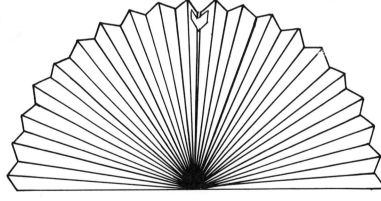

3.
Spread into semicircle.
Staple or tape together
at top.

screen

TO MAKE A HOUSE

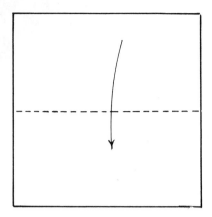

1.
With white side of paper
up, fold square in half.

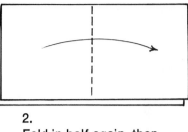

2.
Fold in half again, then
unfold.

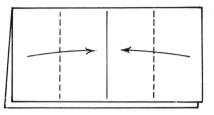

3.
Fold outer edges to
center crease made
before. Unfold.

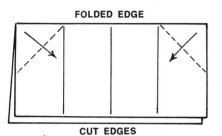

FOLDED EDGE

CUT EDGES

4.
Fold corners to creased lines as shown by dotted lines and arrows. Unfold.

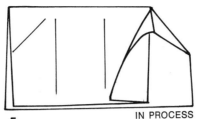

IN PROCESS

5.
Take single top layer of paper at the bottom corner and fold to center crease, at the same time spreading the top into roof shape.

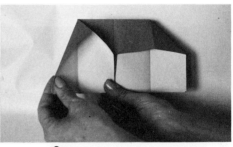

6.
Repeat step 5 on the other side.

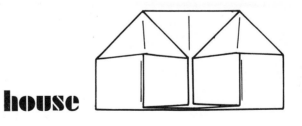

house

The House can be used as a base for making furniture and other things. Some of the possibilities are shown on the following pages. Children enjoy using this furniture and the Table and Bench on page 47 to equip a house made from a grocery box. For this purpose cut off the lid of the box and turn it sideways.

53

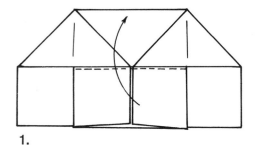

1.
Make the basic House Fold (page 53). Fold center flap up as shown by dotted line and arrow.

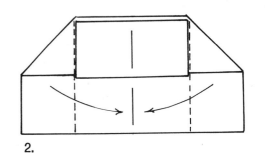

2.
Fold sides to the center as shown by dotted lines and arrows.

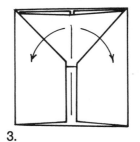

3.
Pull center flap forward as shown so that it is at a right angle to the back. At the same time let the side flaps open up to right angles. See next drawing for how Sofa should look.

54

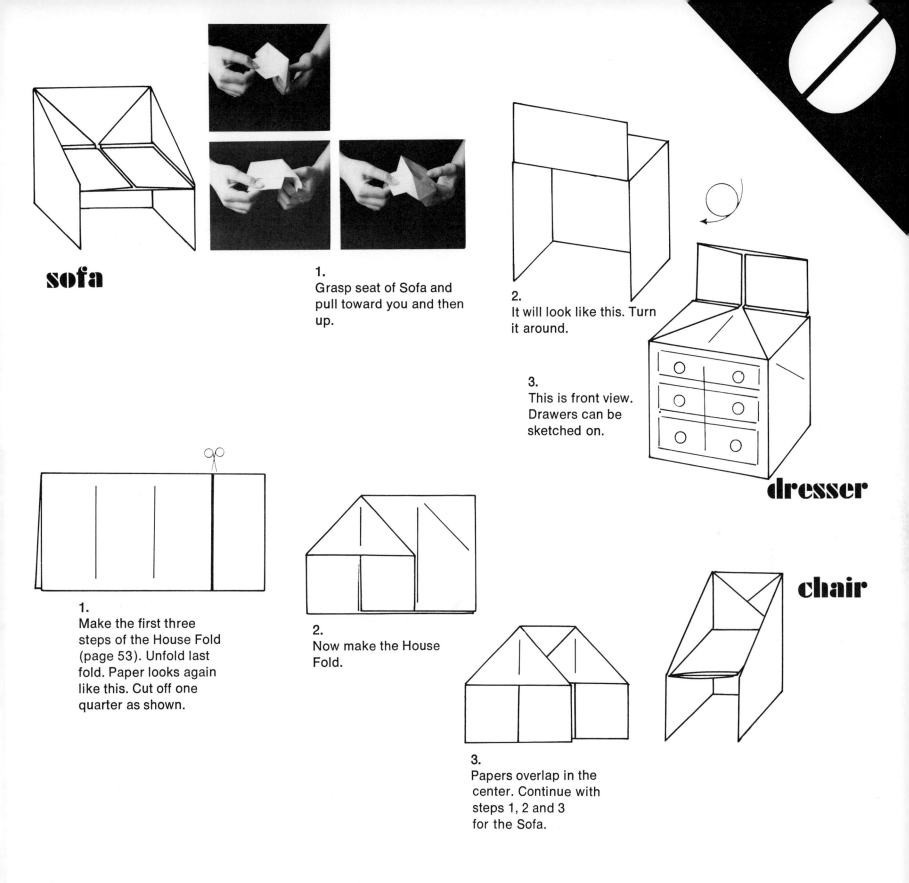

sofa

1.
Grasp seat of Sofa and pull toward you and then up.

2.
It will look like this. Turn it around.

3.
This is front view. Drawers can be sketched on.

dresser

1.
Make the first three steps of the House Fold (page 53). Unfold last fold. Paper looks again like this. Cut off one quarter as shown.

2.
Now make the House Fold.

3.
Papers overlap in the center. Continue with steps 1, 2 and 3 for the Sofa.

chair

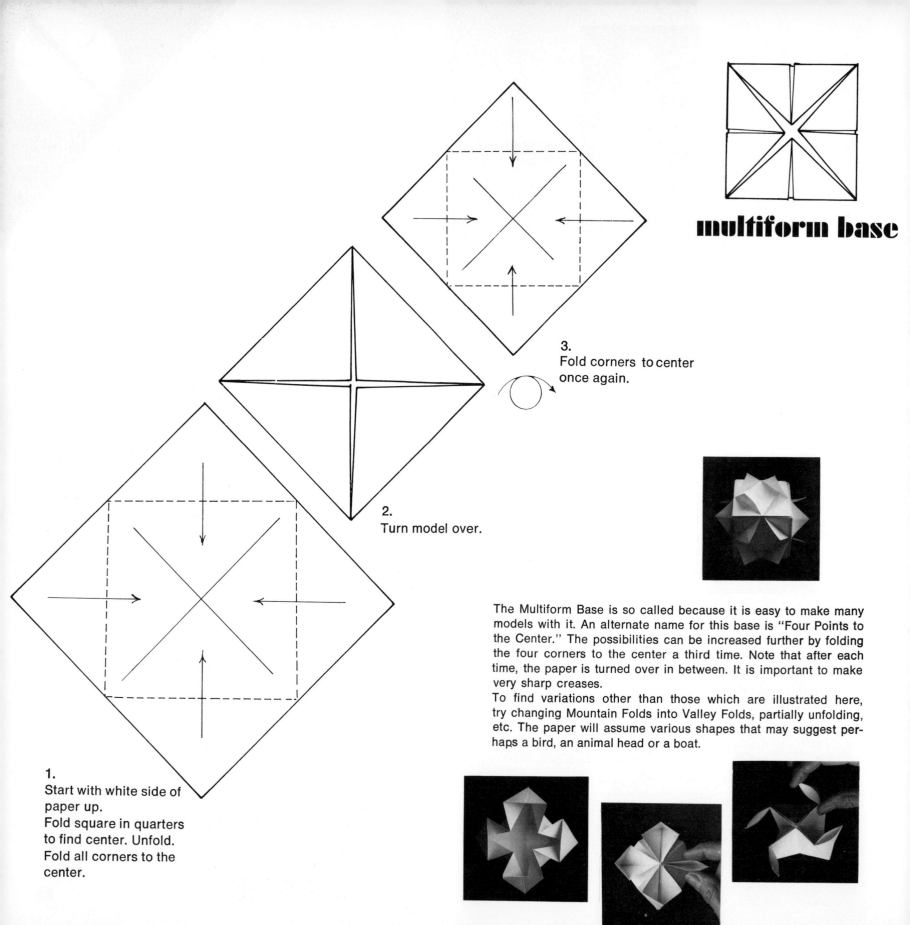

multiform base

3.
Fold corners to center
once again.

2.
Turn model over.

1.
Start with white side of
paper up.
Fold square in quarters
to find center. Unfold.
Fold all corners to the
center.

The Multiform Base is so called because it is easy to make many models with it. An alternate name for this base is "Four Points to the Center." The possibilities can be increased further by folding the four corners to the center a third time. Note that after each time, the paper is turned over in between. It is important to make very sharp creases.

To find variations other than those which are illustrated here, try changing Mountain Folds into Valley Folds, partially unfolding, etc. The paper will assume various shapes that may suggest perhaps a bird, an animal head or a boat.

TO MAKE A COASTER

4.
Turn Multiform Base over.

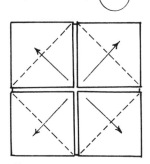

5.
Fold corners outward from center.

coaster

IN PROGRESS

Do not be afraid to squeeze the paper as far as it will go, all the way to the center.
It will spring apart by itself a little bit, to make a Four-Pointed Star of great depth.

6.
The Coaster can be turned into a Three-Dimensional Star with just a little more work.
Insert left thumb into the pocket at one of the corners.
Then squeeze corner together between right thumb and forefinger.
Repeat with other three corners.

7.
The Three-Dimensional Star can be made into a Bird Puppet:
On one corner, fold the single layer of paper down.

bird puppet

star

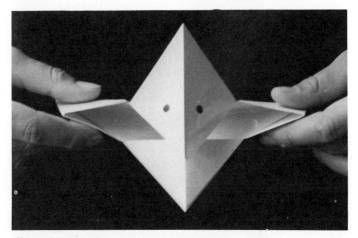

To make Bird Puppet move, grasp two opposite corners and push them toward each other, back and forth.

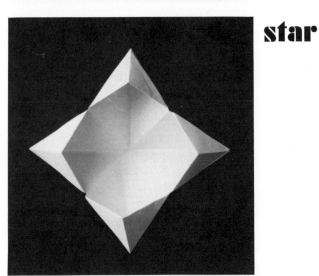

57

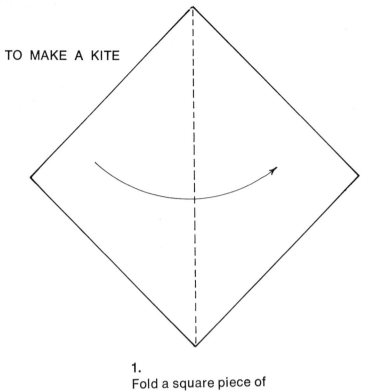

TO MAKE A KITE

1.
Fold a square piece of
paper in half on the
diagonal, then unfold.

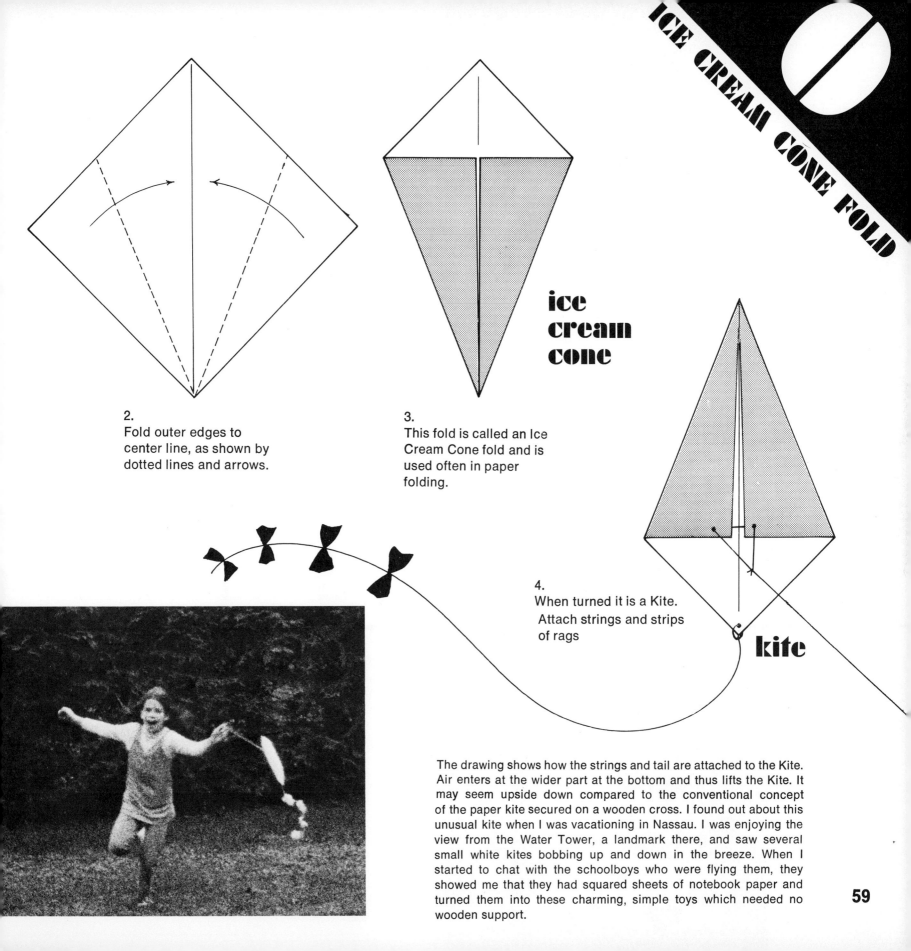

ice cream cone

2.
Fold outer edges to center line, as shown by dotted lines and arrows.

3.
This fold is called an Ice Cream Cone fold and is used often in paper folding.

4.
When turned it is a Kite. Attach strings and strips of rags

kite

The drawing shows how the strings and tail are attached to the Kite. Air enters at the wider part at the bottom and thus lifts the Kite. It may seem upside down compared to the conventional concept of the paper kite secured on a wooden cross. I found out about this unusual kite when I was vacationing in Nassau. I was enjoying the view from the Water Tower, a landmark there, and saw several small white kites bobbing up and down in the breeze. When I started to chat with the schoolboys who were flying them, they showed me that they had squared sheets of notebook paper and turned them into these charming, simple toys which needed no wooden support.

59

TO MAKE A HAT

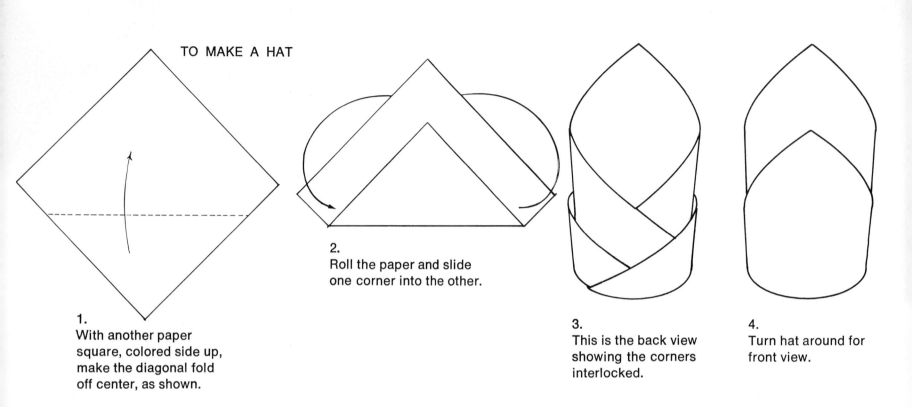

1.
With another paper
square, colored side up,
make the diagonal fold
off center, as shown.

2.
Roll the paper and slide
one corner into the other.

3.
This is the back view
showing the corners
interlocked.

4.
Turn hat around for
front view.

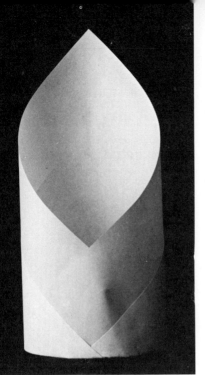

crown/hat

This is easily made from a napkin, paper or fabric. Since it stands up by itself, it adds a lot of color to table setting.

Fold the paper on different angles. You can have a hat shop with many different Hats in no time.

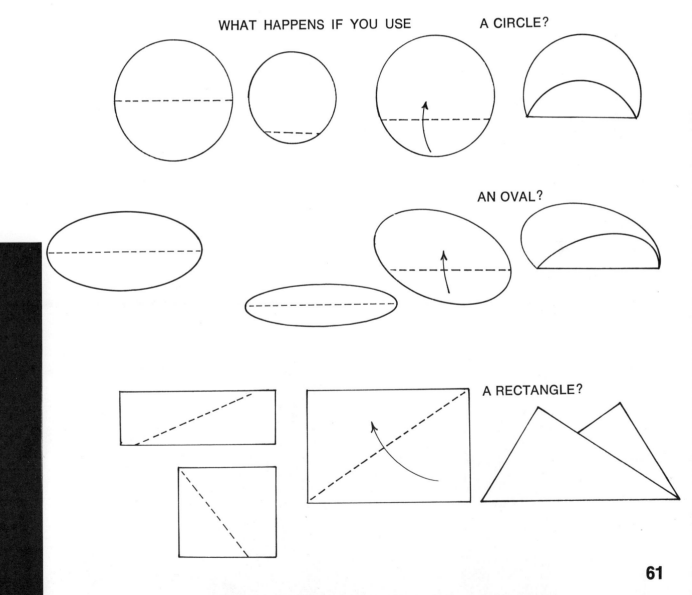

WHAT HAPPENS IF YOU USE   A CIRCLE?

AN OVAL?

A RECTANGLE?

61

TO MAKE A PECKING BIRD

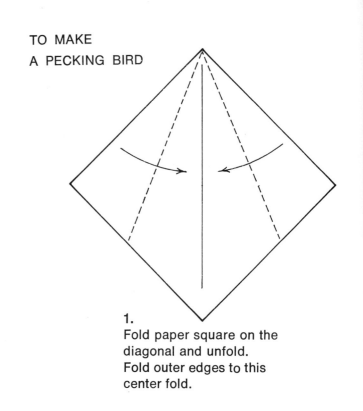

1.
Fold paper square on the diagonal and unfold.
Fold outer edges to this center fold.

Variations developed from the pecking bird.

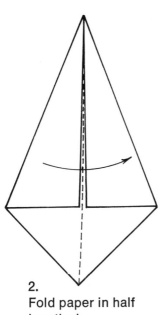

2.
Fold paper in half lengthwise.

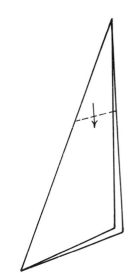

3.
Fold on dotted line in direction of arrow, first to the front and then to the back (Valley and then Mountain).
This is a temporary fold indicating the line for the final reverse fold. Unfold it. Model looks like step 3 again.

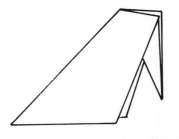

4.
Now grasp beak between thumb and forefinger and place between the two layers of paper. To make the beak stay firmly, recrease the short folds at the back of the head. (The reason why this fold is called the Reverse Fold is that you are reversing the direction of one of these short creases from a Valley Fold to a Mountain Fold.)

pecking bird

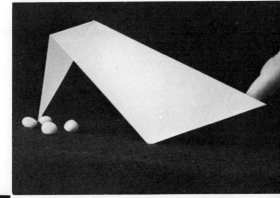

Place bird on a flat surface and tap the tail downward; the bird seems to peck.

The reverse fold is extremely important in origami as it adds a lot of variety. The following steps will show how it is made.
Please practice several of these until you can make a Reverse Fold easily.

INSIDE REVERSE FOLD IN PROGRESS

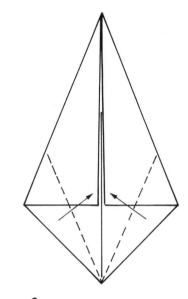

1.
Start the same way as
for the Pecking Bird
(page 63):
Fold square on the
diagonal and unfold.
Make Ice Cream Cone
Folds by folding outer
edges to center fold.

2.
Make Ice Cream Cone
Folds on the lower
points, as shown by
dotted lines and arrows.

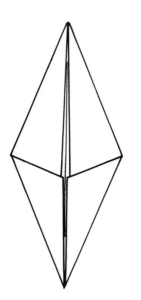

diamond base

TO MAKE A WOODPECKER

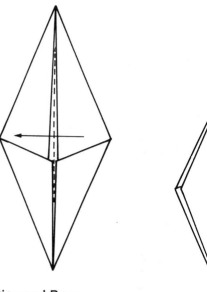

1.
Make a Diamond Base.
Fold in half lengthwise.

2.
Make a Reverse Fold.

woodpecker

65

The Rabbit's Ear Fold is a standard fold used many times and is so called because it produces a long narrow fold which looks like a rabbit's ear. It is made on a triangular area.

TO MAKE A RABBIT'S HEAD MASK

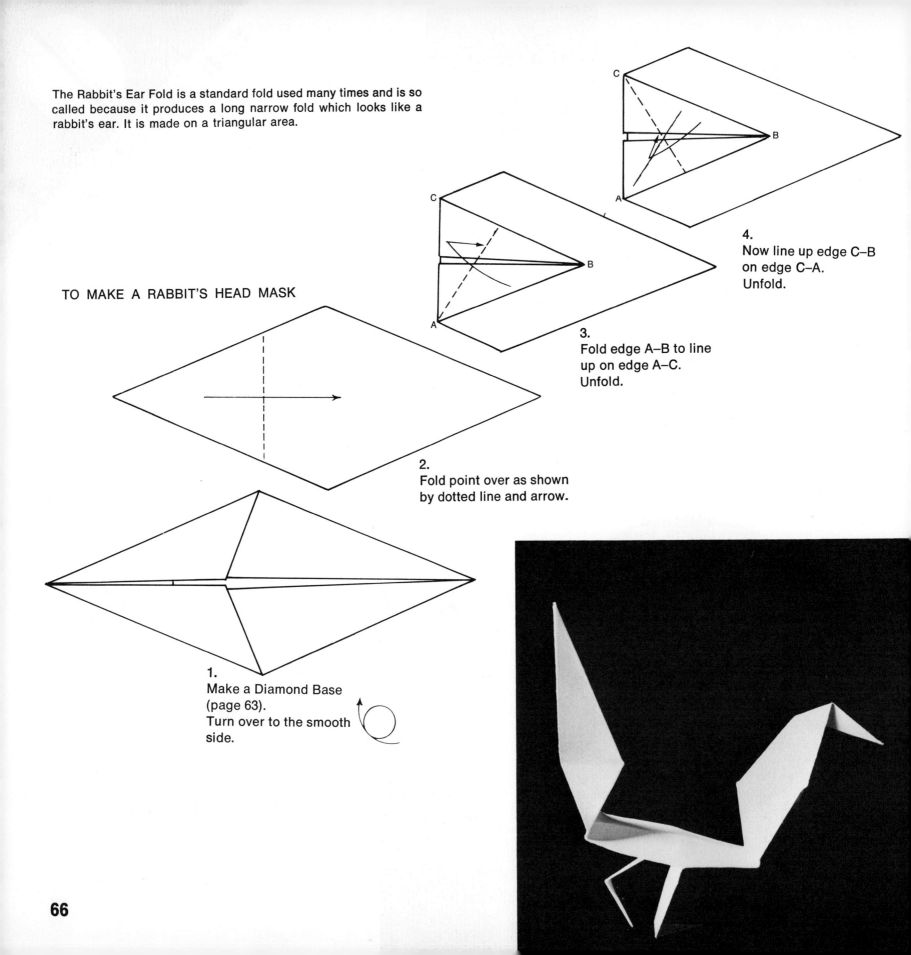

4.
Now line up edge C–B on edge C–A.
Unfold.

3.
Fold edge A–B to line up on edge A–C.
Unfold.

2.
Fold point over as shown by dotted line and arrow.

1.
Make a Diamond Base (page 63).
Turn over to the smooth side.

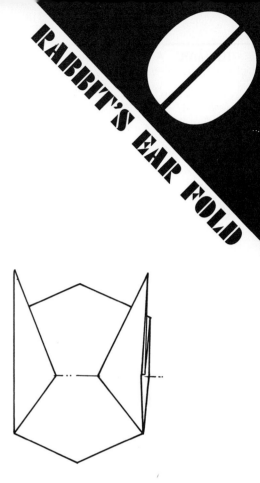
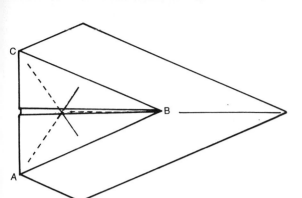

IN PROGRESS

5.
Now pinch edges A–B and B–C toward each other until they meet on the crossed creases you made before. This enables you to flatten the rabbit's ear on the dotted lines to result in the next step.

rabbit's ear fold

6.
This completes one rabbit's ear fold.
To make the second rabbit's ear, fold other point and repeat steps 2, 3, 4 and 5.

7.
Mountain fold the upper half behind, leaving the ears alone.

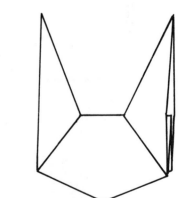

rabbit's head mask

To make a full size mask that can be worn, use a 20″ [50 cm] square of brown wrapping paper. Cut out eyes and attach string or elastic.

TO MAKE A FISH BASE

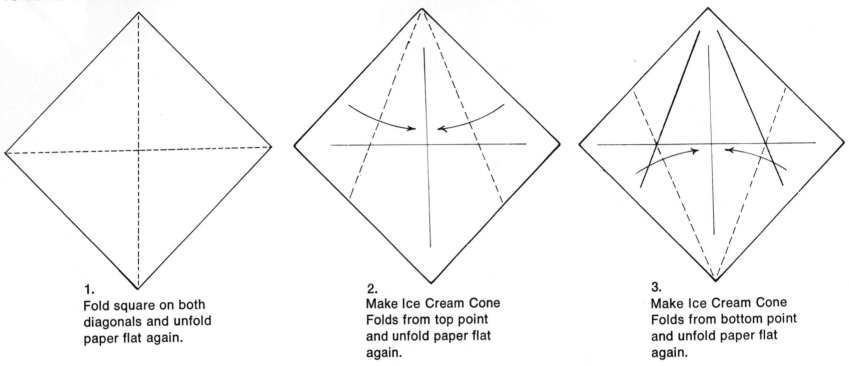

1.
Fold square on both diagonals and unfold paper flat again.

2.
Make Ice Cream Cone Folds from top point and unfold paper flat again.

3.
Make Ice Cream Cone Folds from bottom point and unfold paper flat again.

A mask is created from the fish base by squashfolding the short points.

Fox puppet created by folding fish fins closer to the center of the model.

VARIATIONS

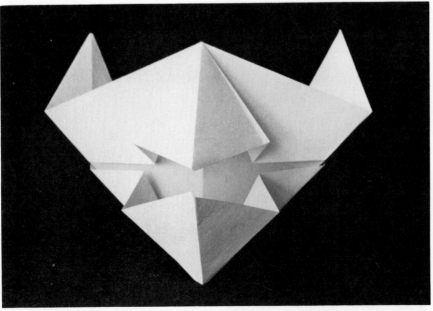

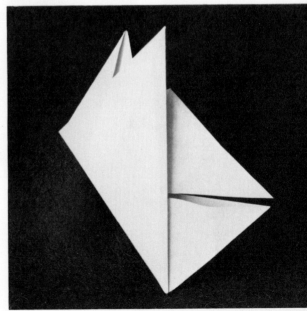

68

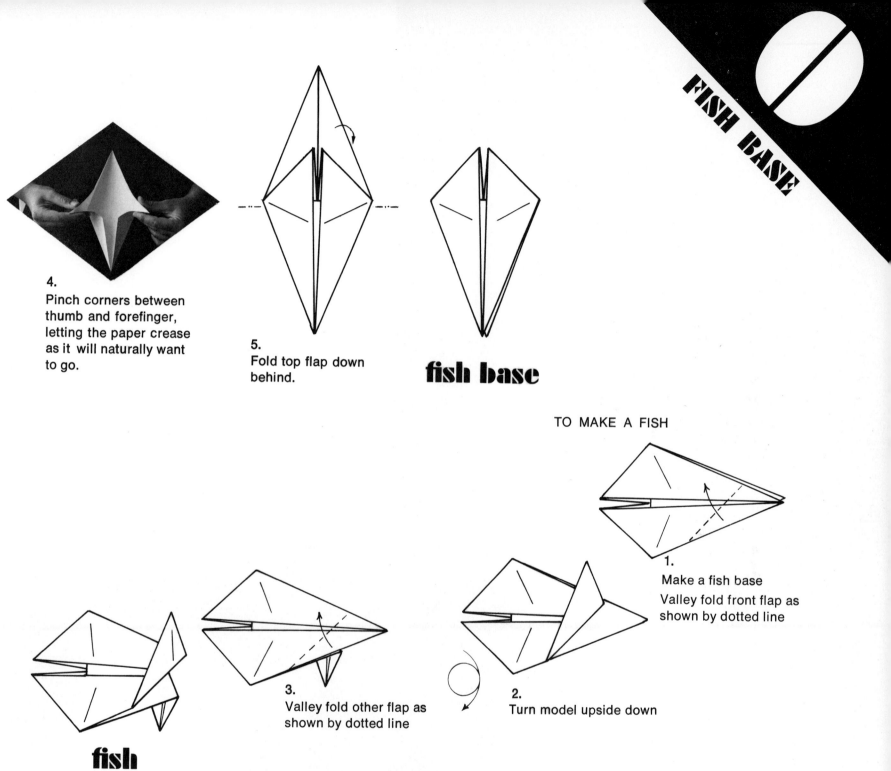

4.
Pinch corners between thumb and forefinger, letting the paper crease as it will naturally want to go.

5.
Fold top flap down behind.

fish base

TO MAKE A FISH

1.
Make a fish base
Valley fold front flap as shown by dotted line

2.
Turn model upside down

3.
Valley fold other flap as shown by dotted line

fish

Grasp one fin with each hand and pull hands away from each other. This makes a breathing fish action toy.

69

TO MAKE A BIRD CANDY DISH

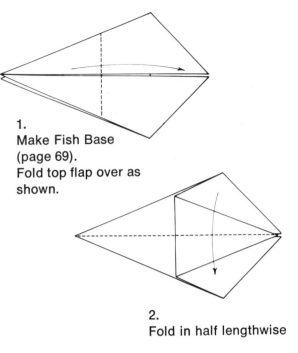

1.
Make Fish Base
(page 69).
Fold top flap over as
shown.

2.
Fold in half lengthwise

**TRY
THESE
VARIATIONS**

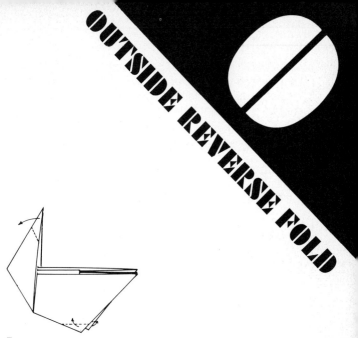

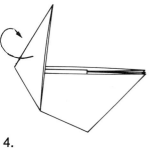

3.
Make an Outside Reverse
Fold for the neck:
As a preparation, fold
on the dotted line.

4.
The neck is now in front
of the main body. To
complete the Outside
Reverse Fold, let the
model open up slightly.
Grasp the neck with the
left hand and place it
around the main body.

5.
Make a small Reverse
Fold for the head. Make
a small fold on each side
of the wings, so that the
dish will stand up well.
Open up wings wide
for the candy.

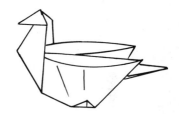

bird candy dish

71

JUSTIFIED CUTTING: The strictest rules of origami do not permit any cutting whatsoever, but sometimes a single cut which enhances a design is permissible. The Shrimp is a good illustration; it would not be as elegant without the long cut feelers.

To make Lobsters, use squares of paper 8″ [20 cm] or larger, and follow the folding steps for the Shrimp.

TO MAKE A SHRIMP

Use a 3″ [8 cm] square of pink paper.
Make a narrowed Diamond Base as follows:

1.
Fold square on diagonal.
Unfold.
Make Ice Cream Cone
Folds as shown by
dotted lines and arrows.

2.
Narrow Ice Cream Cone
by folding on dotted
lines to center.

3.
Make Ice Cream Cone
Folds at other end.

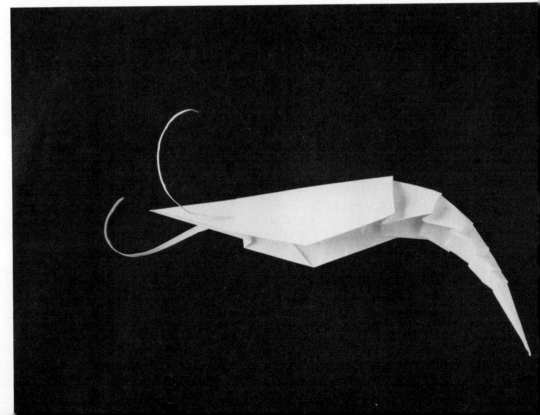

72

4.
Make narrow cuts on the folded edges in the center, as shown. Then make a pleat by making first a Valley Fold, as shown by the dotted line, and then a Mountain Fold close to it.

5.
Cut small triangle snips into the pleat as shown. Then pass feelers through these holes.

6.
Crimping   Make pleats on the body as shown. Each pleat is formed by a Valley Fold and a Mountain Fold close together.

7.
Fold Shrimp in half lengthwise.

8.
Hold body of Shrimp with left hand. Round the tail of the Shrimp by stretching the top of the pleat (see arrows), leaving the bottom part of the pleat closed. Do one pleat at a time. Each one of these angled pleats is a *Crimp*.

shrimp

73

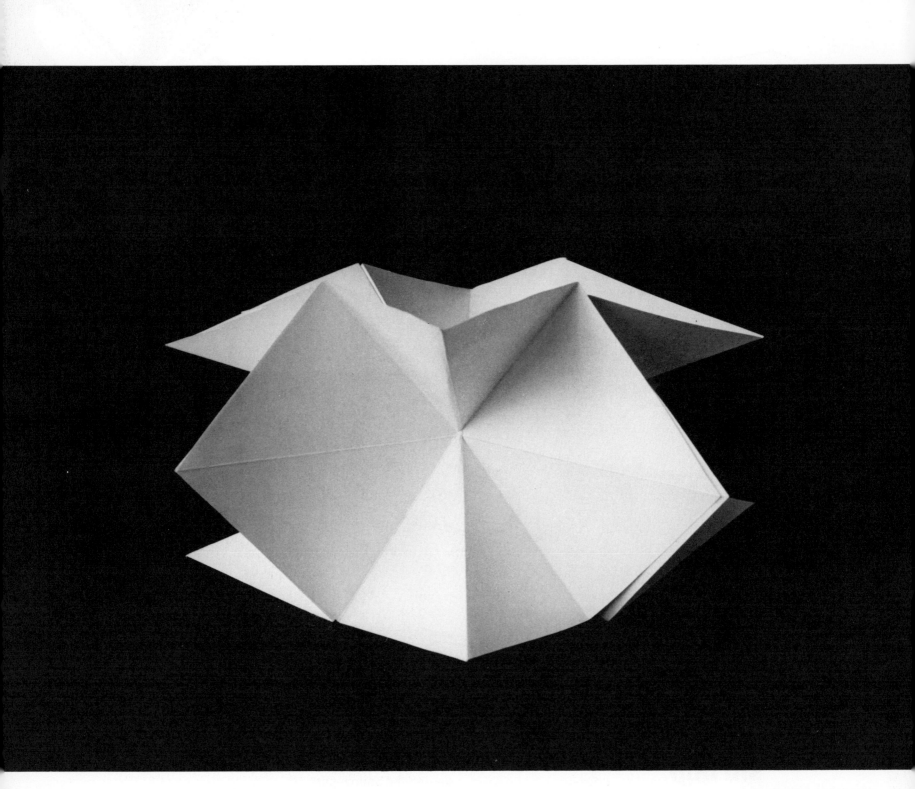

Combination fold of square
and triangle bases, suitable
for a mobile.

TO MAKE A SQUARE BASE

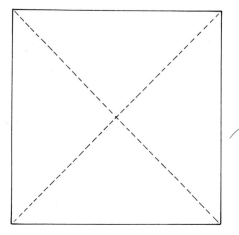

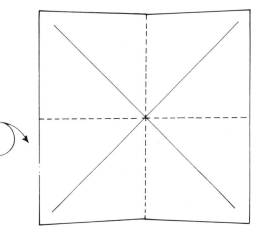

1.
With colored side of
paper up, fold paper on
the diagonals. Unfold.
Turn paper over.

2.
With white side of paper
up now, fold paper in
half. Unfold.
Fold in half in other
direction.

3.
Leaving paper creased
on the last fold, hold it
with fingers in position
exactly as shown and
push gently together
until you have the shape
shown below.

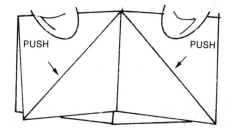

PUSH   PUSH

square base

TO MAKE A WASTEPAPER BASKET

OPEN POINTS

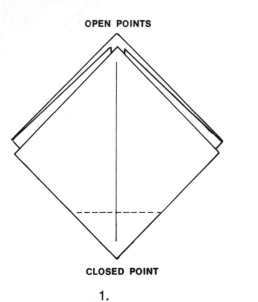

CLOSED POINT

1.
Make Square Base
(page 75). Fold
backward and forward
on dotted line to make a
sharp crease.

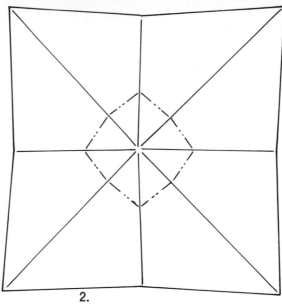

2.
Open up paper and you
will see a small square
in the center. Mountain
fold the little square and
then close up into the
original shape with the
point sunk inside.

IN PROGRESS

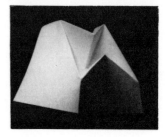

party hat

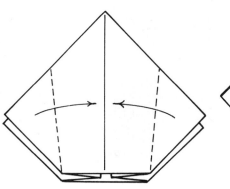

3.
Fold on dotted lines.

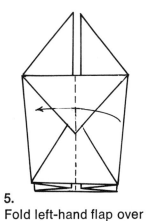

4.
Fold top point down.
Turn model over and
repeat on back.
Top layer only.
Turn model over and
repeat on back.

5.
Fold left-hand flap over
to the right, like a book.
Turn model over and
repeat this on the back.

6.
For added strength, use
cellophane tape. Then
fold top point down.
Turn model over and
repeat on back.

wastepaper basket

The wastepaper basket can be turned
into a basket by stapling on a handle.

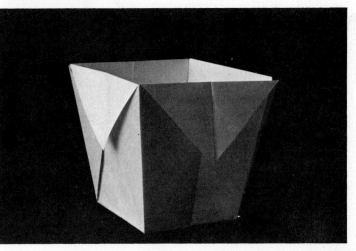

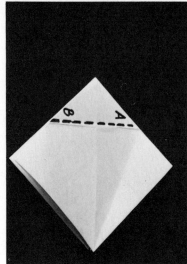 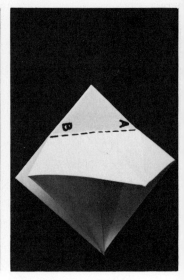

3.
Pick up top layer of
paper only. Lift upward,
fold on dotted line A–B.
As you do this the outer
edges of the paper will
meet in the center.

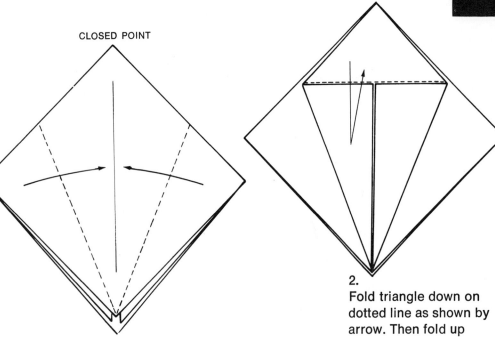

CLOSED POINT

OPEN POINT

1.
Make Square Base
(page 75), and place
with closed point away
from you, as shown.
Top flaps only, fold outer
edges to center line as
shown by dotted lines
and arrows.

2.
Fold triangle down on
dotted line as shown by
arrow. Then fold up
again.

Turn model over and
repeat steps 1 and 2 on
the back. Then unfold
steps 1 and 2. Model
looks again as in drawing
1, but has extra creases
in it.

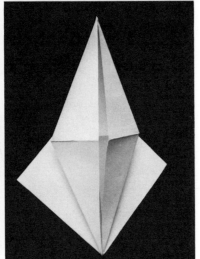

4.
Flatten to make a
diamond shape, as
shown next .
(This step is called a
Petal Fold.)

Turn model over and
repeat on back.

bird base

The Bird Base is the most popular
base for making all kinds of
origami animals because it offers
the greatest possibilities.

Illustrations of two projects made
with the bird base (see pages
81 and 85)

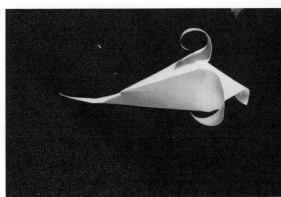

79

TO MAKE A TRADITIONAL CRANE

1.
Make a Bird Base (page 79).
Make Ice Cream Cone Folds as shown. First make two on the front. Turn model over and repeat on the back.

2.
Reverse fold as shown.

3.
Make a Reverse Fold for the head.

4.
Turn bird over. Hold wing in each hand. Pull apart gently and blow into hole at X.

traditional crane

A playful change of the flapping
bird produces a flower or a

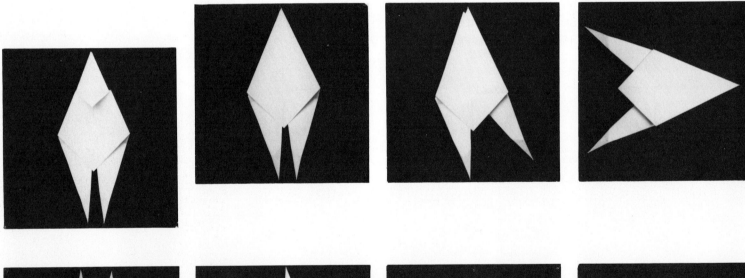

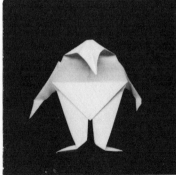

Martian.

TO MAKE A FLAPPING BIRD

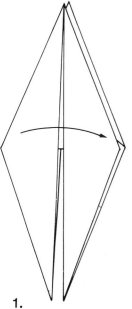

1.
Make a Bird Base
(page 79).
Swing left top flap to the
right in a Book Fold.
Then turn model over
and repeat on back.

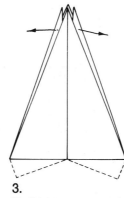

2.
Fold front flap as shown
by dotted line and arrow.
Turn model over and
repeat on back.

3.
Pull hidden point in
direction of arrow.
As you move points out,
paper will spread out
below. Crease sharply
where dotted lines show
to keep folds in position.

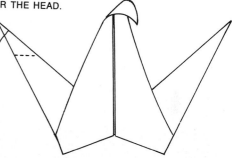

MAKE SMALL
REVERSE FOLD
FOR THE HEAD.

WINGS ARE ROLLED SLIGHTLY.

flapping bird

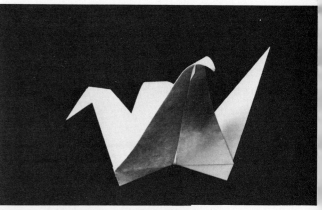

To flap wings hold bird at X with left hand and with right hand move
tail *gently* in direction of arrows back and forth—not up and down.
Sometimes the wings will not flap and it is necessary to relieve
tension at center point Z. To do this grasp one wing as close as
possible to Z with right hand and wiggle it back and forth. Repeat
with other wing.

Bowl of flowers, origami models created by Florence Temko, folded by Alice Grey

84

TO MAKE A FLOWER

1.
Make a Bird Base
(page 79).
Fold front flap only down
as shown by dotted line
and arrow.

2.
Fold short edges to
center.
Turn model upside down
from top to bottom.

3.
Fold outer edges to
center to make stem.

4.
Book fold front flap.

5.
Make a Valley Fold on
the stem for a graceful
curved effect.

6.
Roll all three petals over
a pencil.
As you do this, Flower
becomes three-
dimensional.

flower

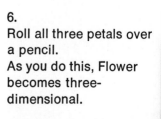

TO MAKE A TRIANGLE BASE

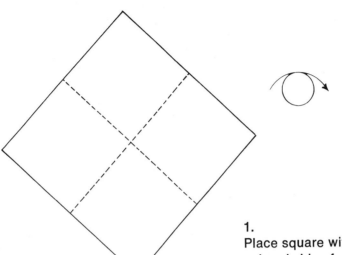

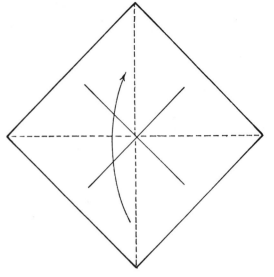

1.
Place square with
colored side of paper up.
Fold on lines as shown.
Unfold.
Turn paper over.

2.
With white side of paper
up, fold on the diagonal.
Unfold. Fold on the other
diagonal. Do not unfold
this time.

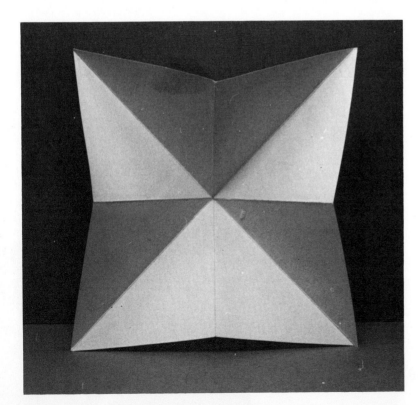

IN PROGRESS

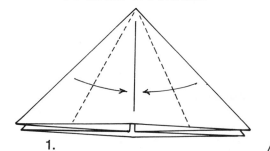

PUSH   PUSH

3.
Hold paper with fingers
in position exactly as
shown and push gently
together until you have
shape shown in final
drawing.

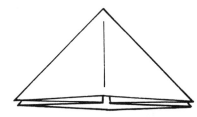

triangle base

called Waterbomb Base

TO MAKE A PYRAMID

1.
Make Triangle Base
Fold outer edges to center.
Turn model over and repeat
on back.

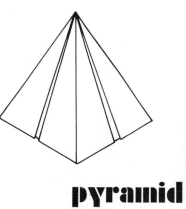

2.
Tuck points inside main
body (Mountain Fold as
shown).

pyramid

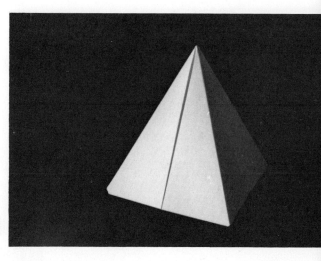

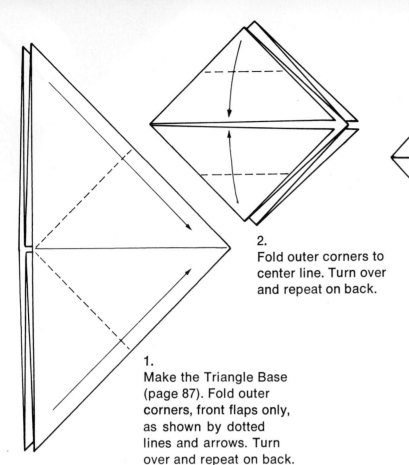

2.
Fold outer corners to center line. Turn over and repeat on back.

3.
Tuck top points into the two pockets shown, front and back. They do not fit all the way into the pockets. See next drawing.
Turn model over. Repeat on back.

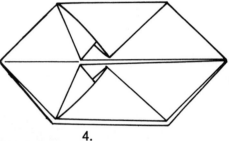

IN PROGRESS

1.
Make the Triangle Base (page 87). Fold outer corners, front flaps only, as shown by dotted lines and arrows. Turn over and repeat on back.

TO MAKE A PAPER BALL

4.
Ball is now completely folded. Inflate it by sliding your forefinger behind the paper as shown. Put your thumb on the outside to hold the folds together. Put other hand on the other side in the same way. Blow into the little hole at the same time as you move your hands gently apart. After it is blown up, the ball may require a little shaping to make it more even.

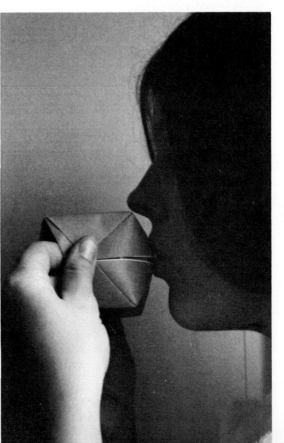

paper ball

TO MAKE A BUD

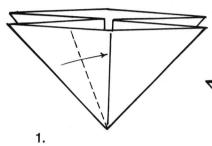

1.
Make Triangle Base
(page 87).
Fold outer edge to the
center line.

2.
Lift the flap and let it
open partially. Squash
flap on top and spread it
evenly over the center
line.

3.
Squash Fold completed
on one flap. Repeat on
all four flaps. You have
to make two Book Folds
to enable you to get to
all four flaps. Bud can be
made in graduated sizes
and hung as a mobile.

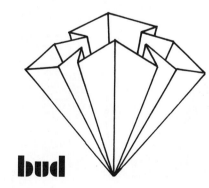

bud

Buds folded in three different
sizes for a mobile.

TO MAKE A FROG BASE

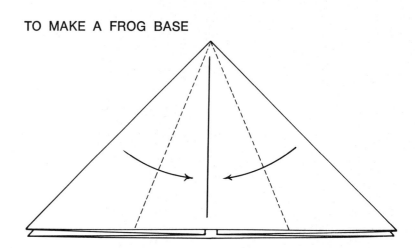

1.
Make Triangle Base (page 87). Fold outer edges to center. Unfold and reverse fold on the same lines.

The Octopus is an illustration of a project made with the frog base. The four legs on the frog (page 93) are cut in half. The resulting eight legs are reverse folded.

TRY
THESE
VARIATIONS
AND
OTHER
PROJECTS

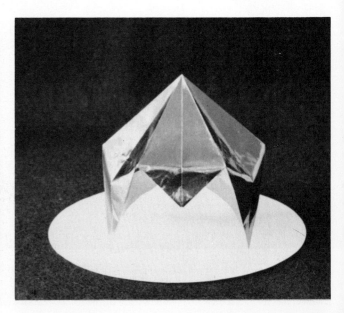

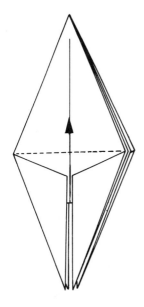

2.
Fold short outer edges
of front flaps to center.
Turn model over and
repeat on the back. Book
fold model front and
back. Again fold outer
edges to the center, front
and back.

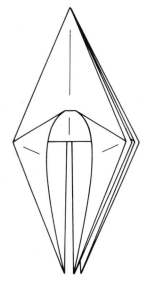

3.
Lift hidden edge in
direction of arrow, and
crease on dotted line.
Sides open up as you do
this.

4.
This shows step 3 in
progress. Turn model
over and repeat on the
back. Book fold model
front and back. Repeat
step 3 front and back.

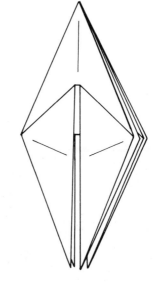

frog base

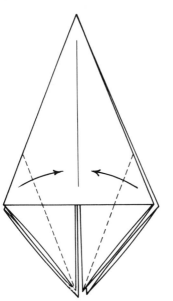

TO MAKE A FROG

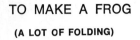

(A LOT OF FOLDING)

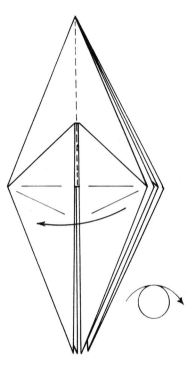

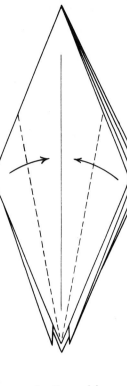

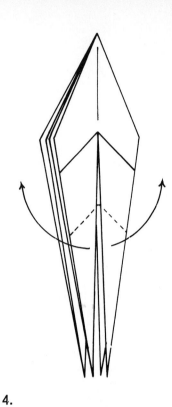

1.
Make a Frog Base (page 91), from green paper. Book fold one flap from the right side to the left. Turn model over and repeat on the back.

2.
Narrow bottom side edges by making Ice Cream Cone Folds as shown. Repeat on all four sides.

3.
Book fold one flap from right side over to the left.
Turn model over and repeat on the back.

4.
There are four separate points here. The two top ones are for the front legs. The other two for the back legs.
Reverse fold top points up, as shown.

92

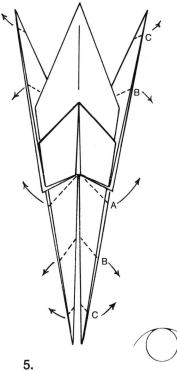

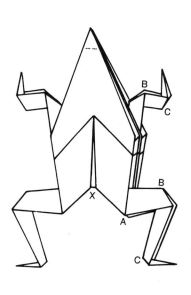

5.
Reverse fold at A, B
and C.
Turn model over.

6.
This drawing shows
Reverse Folds for the
front and back legs.
Valley Fold
front tip.

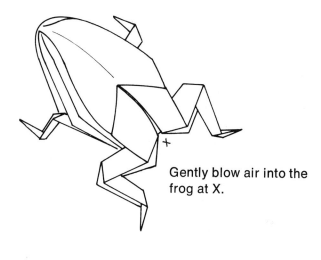

Gently blow air into the
frog at X.

frog

If you make a frog from a 6″ [15 cm]
square and blow in just a little air, you
can make a Jumping Frog. Stroke Frog
sharply with a snapping motion with
your forefinger at X. Frog will jump.

If you make Frog from larger paper and
blow more air into him, he will look like
a real bullfrog, but will not jump.

93

TO MAKE A BOWL

To make a 4″ [10 cm] bowl, you need an 8″ [20 cm] square of paper.

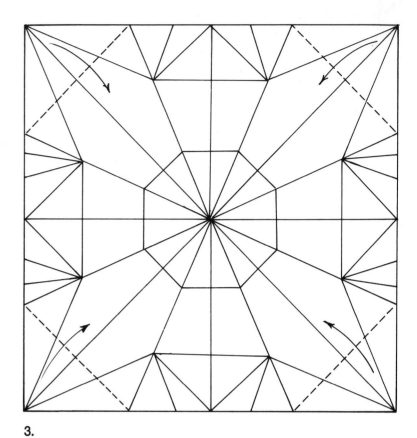

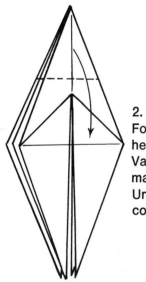

1.
Make a Frog Base (page 93).

2.
Fold top point down to here. First make a Valley Fold. Unfold and make a Mountain Fold. Unfold the paper completely.

3.
Valley fold all four corners toward the center as shown.

bowl

94

4.
Refold the paper into
the Frog Base on the
original creases. (Hint:
First pleat all radii by
alternating Mountain
Folds and Valley Folds,
as shown in drawing.

5.
This crease forms the
bottom of the Bowl.
When you open up the
bowl, recrease the lines
into Mountain Folds as
well as possible.

IN PROGRESS

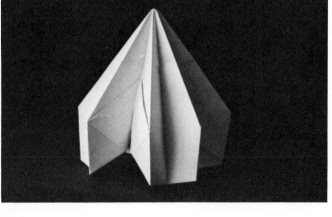

PUSHMI-PULLYU (Advanced)   The Pushmi-Pullyu is an imaginary two-headed animal, a friend of the fictional Dr. Doolittle. To make a Pushmi-Pullyu you need two paper squares. Both are folded the same way, except for the final steps.

1.
Fold each square into a
Frog Base (page 91).

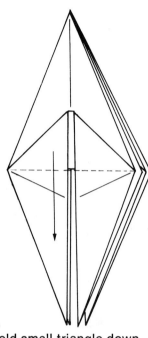

2.
Fold small triangle down.
Repeat on all four flaps.

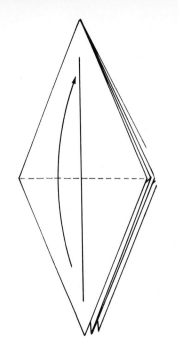

3.
Make a Book Fold by
folding right-hand top
flap to the left. Turn
model over and repeat
Book Fold.

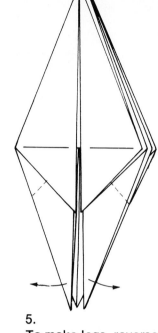

4.
Fold top flap up.

5.
To make legs, reverse
fold two flaps to the
outside as shown.

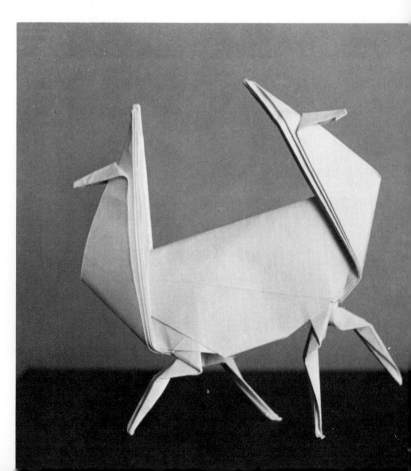

96

6.
Narrow legs by folding
outer edges to center.
You have to open the
flaps to be able to tuck
in edges.

7.
Lift cut edges toward the
outside as far as they
will go. Fold tip up.
Fold model in half
lengthwise.

8.
Make an Outside Reverse
Fold for the neck.

9.
Make a Reverse Fold
for the head of the
inside layer only. Leave
other layer to stand up
as horns.

Narrow one of the bodies
and then slide into the
other body.

Reverse fold legs and
make other slight
adjustments which will
make the Pushmi-Pullyu
look more animated.

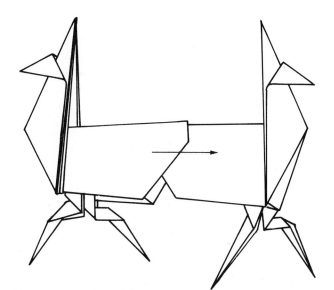

pushmi-pullyu

97

PAPER CUT

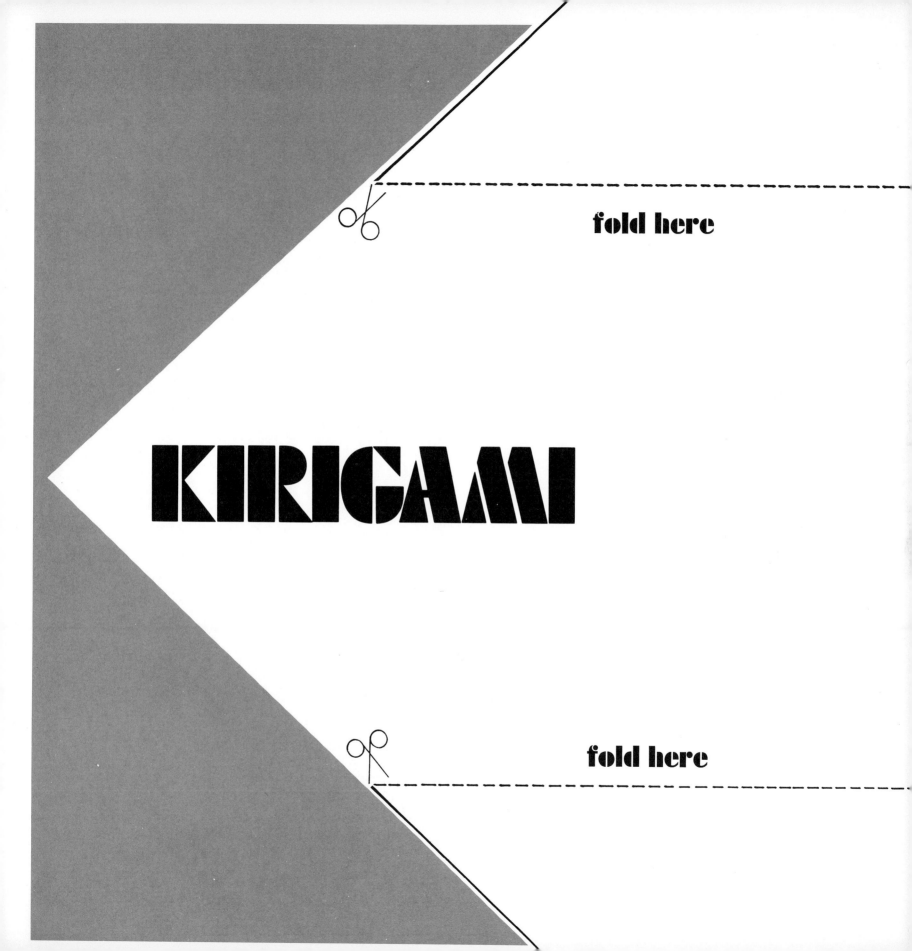

fold here

KIRIGAMI

fold here

KIRIGAMI
CONTENTS

PAPER · CUT KIRIGAMI

Thai Shadow Theater Puppet, cut
from heavy paper

INTRODUCTION

Paper cutting is one of the oldest crafts deeply rooted in many cultures and cutting shapes seems instinctive. Young children love to cut paper and in the hands of experienced artists paper cutting can result in sophisticated works of art. As you try your hand at some of the instructions, you will find that you can draw pictures with scissors or produce surprising trick effects, some of them so spectacular that they could form part of a magician's routine.

Historians relate paper cutting to shadow puppets, pierced silhouette figures made from paper or paperlike materials. Shadow puppet theater survives to a small extent in the Far East and in the Eastern Mediterranean. Chinese puppets are made from translucent animal skins and Javanese puppets, made from thinly shaved wood, dance on a stick. In Greece and Turkey flat, full-length puppets are made from cardboard or felt.

In the nineteenth century, in countries as far apart as China and Switzerland, itinerants entertained with artistic cut-outs. At the same time European and American society was fascinated by a fad for silhouette portraits.

Paper cutting is most widely practiced in China, Mexico and Poland, but it appears sporadically in other countries not prominently known for paper craft. For example, in the United States the Pennsylvania Dutch continued the nineteenth-century European tradition of cut-out valentines and birth and confirmation certificates. These bear a strong resemblance to the stencil painting on furniture and hex signs for which the Pennsylvania Dutch are well known.

Paper cutting is sometimes called kirigami, a word made up of the Japanese *kiri* for cutting and *gami* for paper. This name was actually created by me for an instruction book *Kirigami, the Creative Art of Paper Cutting,* which was included in a kit with paper squares and a pair of scissors. This had such a wide distribution that kirigami became a generic term.

background

Chinese cut-outs, illustrating
different styles prevailing in
various regions.

china

It is in China that the art of paper cutting has reached its highest peak. Paper cut-outs were first mentioned in Chinese writings in the tenth century, but folk arts are not too well documented and it is possible that they were made before that time.

At one time paper cutting ranked with cooking and embroidery as one of the required accomplishments of Chinese girls and in certain regions it was the custom for the bride to present gifts of her work to the bridegroom's family, who judged her critically on her skill.

Most paper cutting is done by housewives for their own use but some farming families augment their incomes by making cut-outs for sale. In the past a small group of people lived only by paper cutting, traveling from town to town, following the same trail as the peddlers, story-tellers, acrobats, scribes and actors, selling their products on the market days.

Thin red tissue paper is used most frequently. To save time, several pieces are threaded together and a pattern is placed on top. Experienced artists cut freehand without a pattern. They use embroidery scissors except when a large number of cut-outs are to be made. In order to turn out as many as fifty, seventy or even one hundred pieces at a time, knives, chisels, needles and other special tools are employed. The stack of paper, held together with thread or nails, is placed in a frame that is covered at the bottom with a resilient emulsion. The design is carved in much the same way as into wood. When the work is completed the sheets of paper adhere to each other from the force of the tools and must be separated very carefully.

The cut-outs are made so precisely that they appear machine made, but sometimes I have seen two examples of the same design and a leaf was angled slightly differ-ently, proving that they came from different handmade batches.

Some families specialize in multicolored paper cuts, assigning different tasks to each member of the family. After the paper is cut, dyes applied to various sections of the paper seep through the many layers. Even a very young child will take part in this labor-saving process and have his own color to cover parts of the design. In Portugal I saw similar family efforts produce colored ceramics.

Chinese paper cutting is closely associated with the week-long New Year's festival when homes are completely redecorated with new paper cuts. They are pasted on walls, ceilings and windows. In the country some windows are made of oiled paper glued onto a wooden lattice frame. This forms a translucent background for the cut-outs, which are popularly called "window-flowers." Paper figures are also placed at the door to protect the home from evil spirits. Other uses are embroidery patterns, hair ornaments and even as witches' talismen for casting evil spells.

The subjects for paper cuts are infinite, obviously drawing on the natural surroundings, birds, bees and butterflies, flora and fauna. Favorite themes include opera stories and legends. The craftsmen repeat age-old motifs and derive creative satisfaction from interchanging them and adding new ones. In today's China, paper cutting is kept alive by the government. New designs include series illustrating the occupations of farmers and soldiers, in keeping with the revolutionary spirit.

An interesting aspect of traditional paper designs is that they are appropriate to the seasons of the year, often symbolic and influenced, like all Chinese art, by calligraphy. Chinese is written in ideographs, which often have double meanings. For example, since the ideograph for a bat is the same as for happiness, whenever a bat appears in a picture it symbolizes happiness. Because the duck and the drake are devoted to each other, the duck is the symbol of marital fidelity. The red color of the paper denotes joy and luck. Traditionally flowers and animals have special meanings. In the same way as the egg is a Christian symbol for Easter, the plum blossom signifies spring, but this kind of symbolism is much more pervasive in the Chinese culture. All this adds a level of meaning to Chinese art not easily appreciated by Westerners, but the beauty can be enjoyed by anyone regardless of his background. The illustrations give you some idea of the lively charm of this folk art.

japan: family crests

In Japan it has been the custom for centuries for an aristocratic family to have a distinctive crest, similar to the English and European coat of arms. The crest is used on all their possessions and in times of war it was easy to identify friend or foe by the crest on the armor or clothing. To this day a kimono may be decorated with a family, company or hotel crest on the front and back, as well as on both sleeves.

Mon-kiri, the art of cutting these crests (translation: *mon* = crest, *kiri* = cutting), is taught in Japanese schools, along with origami. Paper squares are used flat, folded once or several times through the center point and then cut.

Japanese Crests

mexico

Mexico's profusion of popular arts expresses the Mexican love of color and fantasy. There is a close relationship between all Mexican folk arts, whether they employ reeds, clay, bread, yarn, tin, paper or any other medium. The same Indian- and Spanish-inspired motifs appear throughout.

Characteristic Mexican decorations are the piñatas. They are made by pasting bright curly paper strips onto clay pots to give them the shape of animals, birds or fruit. During the nine-day holiday season preceding Christmas Day, it is a game for young and old to be blindfolded and beat a suspended piñata with a stick. When the piñata is finally broken, everyone scrambles for the sweetmeats and toys which tumble out.

Equally charming are the imaginative paper cuts which are produced in four main localities, but appear all over Mexico. There are four different types:

> Tissue paper flags and pictures
> Fertility figures
> Bark paper cut-outs
> Crepe paper flowers

The tissue paper flags are usually 8″ x 6″ [20 cm x 15 cm]; the pictures vary in size up to 3′ [90 cm]. About thirty sheets of tissue paper are covered with a single sheet of heavier paper and all tied together in the two top corners. To prevent the stack of paper from shifting, the edges and some inside areas are secured with rows of pins. After the artist draws his design on the top sheet, he is ready for cutting out. He uses a collection of scissors and handmade cutting tools. Although the method of cutting is similar to Chinese paper cutting, the style is entirely Mexican. The pictures are as varied as Mexican life. Some may depict folk heroes wearing large sombreros and carrying guitars

Mexican decorative panel
approximately 3′ x 2′
(1 m x 65 cm)

Mexican Magic Figure made
from amatl bark paper

110

to serenade their ladies. Other favorite subjects are scenes from nature or legend, flowers, peacocks and other animals, angels and birds. Skeletons and skulls are themes that appear frequently for All Souls' Day, November 2nd. This is an important holiday, combining a serious and mocking attitude toward death. It is an ancient belief that the souls of the dead return on this day to visit their graves and partake of the elaborate meal which is part of the celebration.

Local fiestas are enlivened by flags strung in the streets, in courtyards and along ceilings, or pinned on fruit in bowls. Paper-cut pictures are used as church decorations, but are equally popular for bars.

Another custom is placing fertility figures in the fields as a prayer for a good harvest. They are made by a special method found only in Mexico. Two layers of white paper are sandwiched between two layers of colored tissue and held together with a few stitches. Before being cut, the paper is folded in half to produce symmetrical cut-outs. Color and design are related to the crop. For example, a yellow figure, with arms raised in supplication and corn cobs at the side, is intended for a corn field.

The magic figure illustrated here and the mat illustrated on page 132 are made from *amatl,* a coarse type of bark paper. It dates back to pre-Colombian days and is similar to *tapa* paper made in the Pacific islands and to African bark cloth. *Amatl* is intimately related to religious beliefs, magic and witchcraft in the remote villages of the Pueblo mountains where life continues in centuries–old ways. The magic figures are made by sorcerers to cast a spell and the color of the paper is always appropriate to the spell. A doll buried near an enemy's home with the intent to harm him is dark brown. Light tan is for love spells and medium brown against sickness.

Crepe paper flowers are a relatively new product of Mexico. These large showy flowers are about 12″ [30 cm] in diameter and provide an instant flash of color, whether they are used for parties or home decorations.

Paper Cutting Artist in traditional Polish costume

Polish Circular Cut-out

Paper cut-out portrait of a Polish paper cutting artist, with sheep shearing scissors commonly used for this craft.

poland

Before the age of television young Polish women amused themselves by spending wintry evenings together cutting paper. They depicted what they saw in their daily lives: farm animals, crowing cocks, doves and trees, framed with stylized ribbons and flowered wreaths as part of the cut-out. Besides conventional rectangular pictures, cut-outs were composed in three-foot-long panels, or in circular forms called stars. All pictures were used to decorate walls, ceilings and furniture and sometimes placed between the double window panes, where they shared the space with sandbags intended to keep out icy drafts. The paper cut-outs were renewed each spring, usually at Easter and the year-old ones were carefully transferred to brighten up the barn.

Since the beginning of the nineteenth century, paper cutting has been a deeply ingrained folk art in Poland, but it was most widely practiced between 1870 and 1890. Although the art originated in Warsaw, it enjoyed its greatest popularity in the country villages. Various regions specialized in different designs. The Kurpie region is famous for symmetrical compositions cut from a folded sheet of paper. Its most distinctive feature is the *leluja,* or Kurpie tree. The main outlines and interior cuts are made first and then ornamental leaves are cut on the edges. Another famous area is Lowic. Here a multicolored effect is produced by pasting ever smaller pieces of paper on top of each other, making as many as four layers.

A lesser known type of Polish paper work is the interweaving of several pieces of paper in different colors. It is hard to believe that the customary tool for cutting out these delicate traceries is a heavy pair of sheep shearing scissors.

Paper cut-outs were intended for personal home use, but talented women sold some of their work to friends and neighbors. During the last twenty years the Polish government has encouraged artists to keep this folk art alive by selling the work in special stores in Poland as well as in a few major foreign cities. As a result the bold and colorful Polish paper cut pictures have found their way into modern homes and apartments all over the world where they blend well with contemporary interiors.

Scene Scherenschnitt, by Walter von Gunten, American, who brought this art from Switzerland.

scherenschnitte

Scherenschnitte is a German word which means scissor cuts. They are finely detailed pictures cut from black paper or sometimes a combination of two different colored papers. Gummed paper may be used for convenience. Favorite subjects include animals, forest and farm scenes and fairy tales, sometimes composed into heart shapes rather than the more conventional rectangles.

It is believed that Scherenschnitte are related to the shadow plays of ancient Egypt. The earliest European Scherenschnitte can be traced back to 1631 in Germany and it is known that seventeenth century carpenters used paper cuts for making stencils for painting and carving furniture decorations. Other paper cuts were made into birth certificates, love letters and New Year's greeting cards. Paper cutting is still taught in some schools in Germany, Switzerland and Austria.

Although women are usually more adept at using scissors, in Switzerland Scherenschnitte were traditionally the work of men. Johann Hauswirth was a giant of a man who lived in the mid-nineteenth century and traveled from farm to farm, exchanging paper cuts for board and lodging. His creations were treasured and preserved in family Bibles.

Quite by chance I met a present-day paper cutter, Christian Schwizgebel, who is a forestry official in a village near Gstaad, in Switzerland. I had seen an advertisement for a concert which was illustrated with a beautiful paper cut-out and inquired about the artist. I was told he lived nearby and that I could easily recognize his house by the unusual wood carving decorations. Fortunately he was at home and not only did he receive me cordially, but took a piece of black paper, folded it in half and, in minutes, cut out the lovely scene above.

It is difficult to imagine how it is possible to cut such complicated designs. Does the artist draw on the design first? Actually, most of the cut-outs are done freehand. The beginner cuts out simple designs with which he becomes familiar through repetition. They are usually delightful in themselves, and he adds more figures to his repertoire over a period of years, combining them in many different ways. If the craft appeals to him and he has an artistic talent, he is able to delight us with the fine paper cuts illustrated here.

Self-portrait by August Edouart,
considered the greatest artist of
silhouette portrait cutting, circa 1828.

the silhouette: a forerunner of photography

When the word silhouette is mentioned it conjures up an old-fashioned black profile portrait. Before the age of photography this was a way to obtain a personal likeness in a short period of time. The methods for making silhouettes were either "cut and pasted" or "hollow."

In the cut and pasted method the head is cut out of black paper in profile and pasted on a white background; the hollow cut method is opposite. The profile is cut as a hole into white paper and pasted on to a black background.

Silhouettes were at the height of popularity in the eighteenth century and are named after Etienne de Silhouette (1709–1767), an unpopular French Minister of Finance who loved to make paper cut portraits. The use of his name was intended to be derogatory to show the disdain of aristocrats for these cheap miniatures. Even when silhouettes became a raging fad in France and Germany, the name of the disliked tax collector remained attached to them. They were frequently mentioned in correspondence, prose and poetry, as status symbols and family games, indicating that they were really part of everyday life. During and after the French Revolution silhouette shapes were hidden in posters and prints as underground political messages. In Germany silhouette cutting was a parlor game. The famous poet, Goethe (1749–1832), and his friends were silhouette enthusiasts. They vied to produce the most artistic and lifelike portraits of each other and welcomed the visits of strangers as a new challenge to their talents.

Mechanical means to facilitate silhouette cutting were developed whereby a shadow cast by a strong light could be traced and cut easily.

Silhouettes were also very popular in England and records show that, as early as 1699, a woman artist by the name of Pyburg made such portraits of the reigning monarchs, William and Mary.

Several New England silhouettists advertised their work in newspapers in the Boston area in the early nineteenth century and are known to have produced thousands of "shades," as they were commonly known.

Master James Ronnie Swinton and Donald, Silhouette in cut black paper by August Edouart. Courtesy Crown Copyright, Victoria and Albert Museum, London

paper cutting in modern art

Some modern artists have turned to paper as a medium to express themselves, often as part of a collage. The influence of paper cutting can sometimes be observed in sheet-metal sculptures and felt collages, as artists adapt paper cutting techniques to other materials.

The commercial artist likewise uses paper cutting as one of many tools of his profession. He cuts tissue paper with an X-Acto knife and pastes down the forms with rubber cement. Many of the advertisements, illustrations, fabrics and graphics that we see every day have been designed in this manner. This method of paper cutting is really drawing with a knife. Any reader interested in learning more about this technique should experiment with an X-Acto knife, beginning with simple shapes and progressing wherever his drawing ability leads him.

materials

Almost any kind of paper is suitable for paper cutting. When a particular kind is required for a project, this is mentioned in the text. In general, colored art paper, origami paper, tissue paper, typewriter paper, newspaper and kitchen foil fill most needs. Local newspaper plants can usually provide leftover ends of newsprint rolls, which are useful for working on a large scale.

Experiment with different weights of paper. For cutting on folded paper, lightweight paper is preferable, but stand-up animals require a heavier substance. Sometimes the thickness affects the results, in the stretch paper technique, for example.

Finished models can be sprayed with Krylon or other plastic finishes for greater durability.

tools

All the designs shown in the paper cutting section of this book can be made with scissors or any X-Acto knife.

SCISSORS MUST BE SHARP   Beyond that every person develops a preference for a certain pair of scissors. It is best to experiment with different scissors until you feel comfortable with a particular pair. My favorite is a blunt-pointed pair with 5½" [14 cm] blades, which I use for everything except small inside cuts. For that purpose I have a pair of embroidery scissors 3¼" [8 cm] long overall. Curved cuticle scissors may suit you and can be held with the curve toward you or away from you. Fiskars scissors from Finland are available for left-handers.

how to mount paper cut-outs

Sobo or Elmer's glue is the most satisfactory. For best results, put a small amount in a saucer or small bowl. Apply it with your forefinger.

Make sure the glue touches only your forefinger and the part of the cut-out you are working on. Keep all other areas clean with a small rag.

Paper cuts made on folded paper should be unfolded just before you are ready to mount them.

METHOD 1:
I observed a Polish folk artist using this method and find it the most satisfactory.

Place paper cut on the surface to which it is to be glued. Hold it down with one hand at the same time as you lift up one corner.

Apply glue to this corner with the forefinger of the other hand.

Continue this procedure, working from one edge of the paper cut toward the opposite edge, glueing down small areas at a time.

METHOD 2:
Place cut-out face down on a piece of newspaper. Apply glue to the back, sparingly.

Lift edges of cut-out with point of scissors. This enables you to lift up the paper cut and transfer it to the surface on which it is to be mounted.

METHOD 3:
If you want to try out different placements for the cut-out, use rubber cement. Page 172 gives information about how to use it.

A cut-out picture by Ugo Mochi.
He calls it a paper sculpture,
which suggests three-dimensional form,
in contrast to silhouette cutting,
which emphasizes shadow outline.

graphic symbols

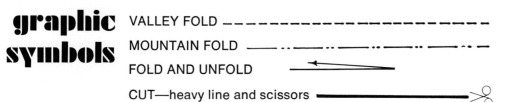

VALLEY FOLD — — — — — — — — — — — — — — — — —

MOUNTAIN FOLD — — ·· — — ·· — — ·· — — ·· — ·· —

FOLD AND UNFOLD ———————→

CUT—heavy line and scissors ━━━━━━━━━━━━✂

procedures

helpful cutting hints

When cutting curves or angles, feed the paper into the scissors. Hold the scissors still and move only the hand holding the paper.

When cutting straight lines, keep both hands more or less in the same position as you squeeze scissors together.

Practice cutting curves and angles at random without a definite design until it becomes natural to move the paper into the scissors.

When using a pair of scissors with long blades, CUT WITH THE PART OF THE BLADES NEAR THE CROSS OF THE SCISSORS to give the greatest control.

straight cutting

When putting scissors to paper, most people find it easiest to make straight cuts.

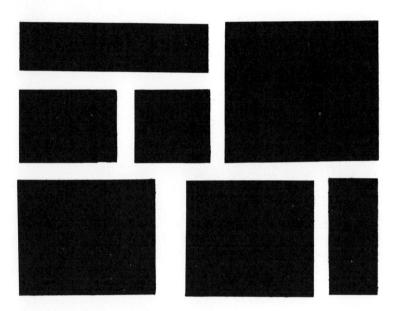

This rectangle cut apart is reminiscent of a modern painting.

A paper square can be cut into geometric shapes which are then presented as a puzzle to be arranged into the original square.

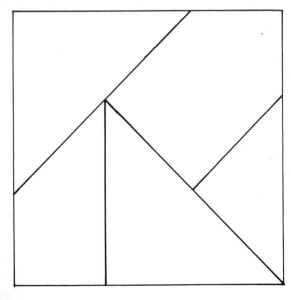

Now using a complete circle, it is first cut in half and then into wedges.

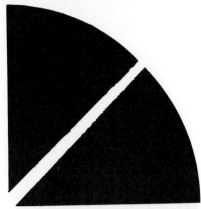

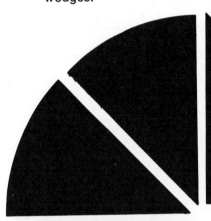

An exercise for training
the eye is to arrange
several such cut-up
circles in different ways.
It soon becomes
apparent that some
results are more pleasing
than others, thus
encouraging the
development of design
abilities.

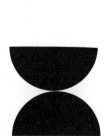

123

curved and interior cutting

Cutting curved shapes is good practice for feeding the paper into the scissors (see page 121). For the blades of grass, curved cuts are made from the top edge of the paper. The inside cuts are made by piercing with small embroidery scissors and then cutting around the holes.

You may discover that the scissors do not always want to follow penciled lines, but are inclined to make a more comfortable and smoother path for themselves. After some practice it becomes easier to cut directly into the paper without first drawing the design.

In selecting an animal or a plant for cut-outs, a moment is well spent thinking about the profile. Does it have a characteristic feature? A rooster is easily recognized by its comb and tail feathers and the snail's house atop its long body makes it simple to portray. Inspiration for many other designs can be found in magazines, encyclopedias and particularly in advertisements.

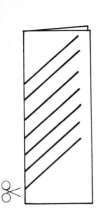

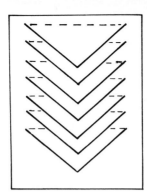

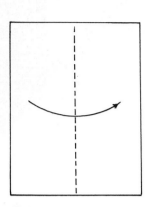

Fold paper in
half lengthwise.

Make diagonal parallel
cuts from the folded
edge, not quite reaching
the opposite cut edges.
Unfold.

Fold points upward
on dotted line.

Many variations are possible. Here every other triangle is folded up
and flattened, creating an entirely different pattern. Paper colored
white on one side and strong color on the other side can be used,
but if this is not available, two pieces of contrasting paper can be
pasted together. Cuts can also be curved or zig-zagged.
Result can be pasted to a piece of contrasting paper for a wall
hanging or a gift wrap decoration.

     This symmetrical cut-out was sug-
gested by Swiss Scherenschnitte. Sections are cut away; enclosed
areas were first pierced with the point of the scissors. It is best to
start working on small pieces of paper and make simple designs.
As you quickly gain confidence, you will sense which designs are
most pleasing.

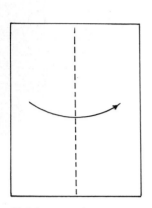

Fold paper in
half lengthwise.

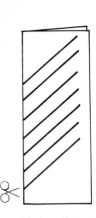

Make diagonal parallel
cuts from the folded
edge, not quite reaching
the opposite cut edges.
Unfold.

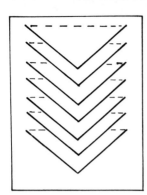

Fold points upward
on dotted line.

Many variations are possible. Here every other triangle is folded up
and flattened, creating an entirely different pattern. Paper colored
white on one side and strong color on the other side can be used,
but if this is not available, two pieces of contrasting paper can be
pasted together. Cuts can also be curved or zig-zagged.
Result can be pasted to a piece of contrasting paper for a wall
hanging or a gift wrap decoration.

This symmetrical cut-out was sug-
gested by Swiss Scherenschnitte. Sections are cut away; enclosed
areas were first pierced with the point of the scissors. It is best to
start working on small pieces of paper and make simple designs.
As you quickly gain confidence, you will sense which designs are
most pleasing.

dog

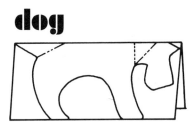

The animals are made
from a basic fold to
which the characteristics
of different species are
applied.

lion

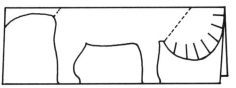

*The Mexican fertility
figure is an example
of a silhouette cut on
paper folded once.*

fantasia

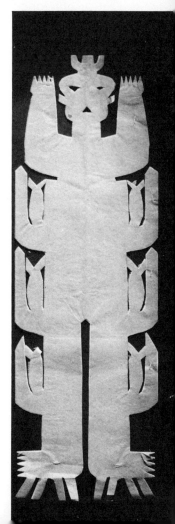

alligator

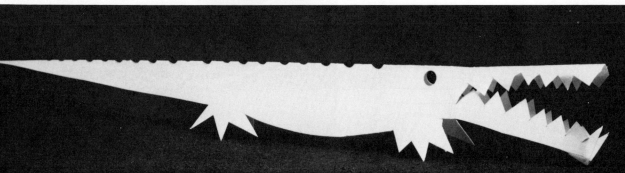

The most intriguing paper cutting is done on folded paper, which multiplies any design. Here are some cutting ideas applied to folded paper:

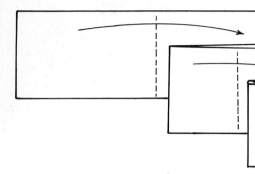

Probably one of the best-known paper cut-outs is paper dolls, which are made from folded paper. To hold them together, part of the opposite edge must remain.

They can be used in three-dimensional displays, standing in a line or arranged in a circle. Boys and girls can be cut out in a single chain, by drawing the half outline of the

Leftover bits from making dolls and chains are useful for collages and decorating greeting cards.

Cuts made alternately from one edge and then from the opposite edge (but never all the way across), permit the paper to be expanded beyond its original size, in lacy patterns.

stretch paper

FOLDED EDGE

paper dolls

boy against one edge and the half outline of the girl on the opposite edge. The method is equally suitable for animals and geometrics.

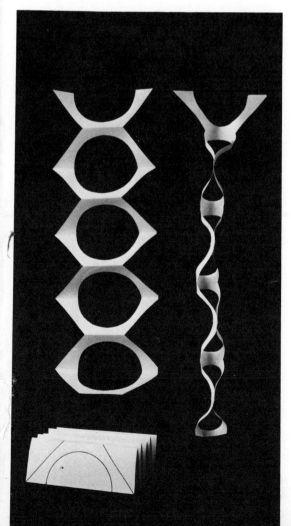

Chains can be made by accordion pleating a long strip of paper or adding machine tape. This pattern results in a chain. It can be made three-dimensional by rolling each segment. Then glue A to B.

chains

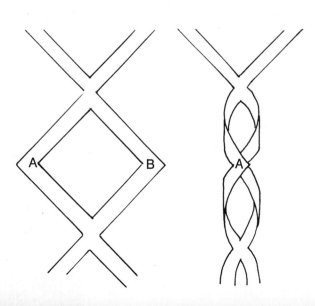

A   B   A

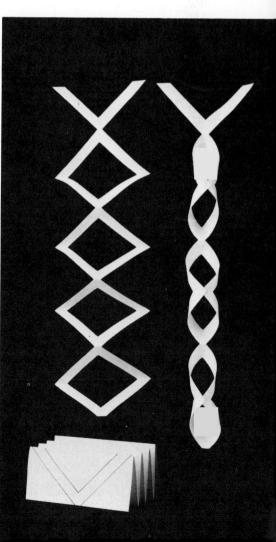

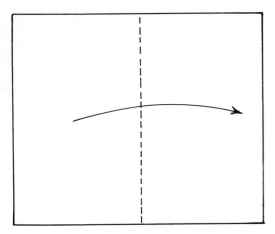
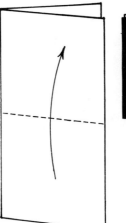

frame

Use a piece of paper the
same size as the outer
dimensions of the
finished frame.

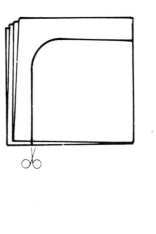
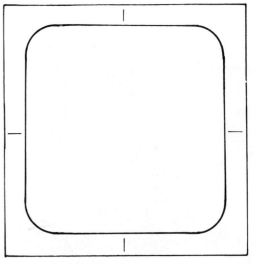

mobile

Bring the two opposite
edges together.
Note the different effect
achieved when you hang
it upside down.

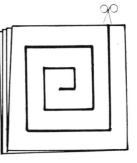

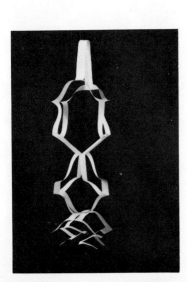

130

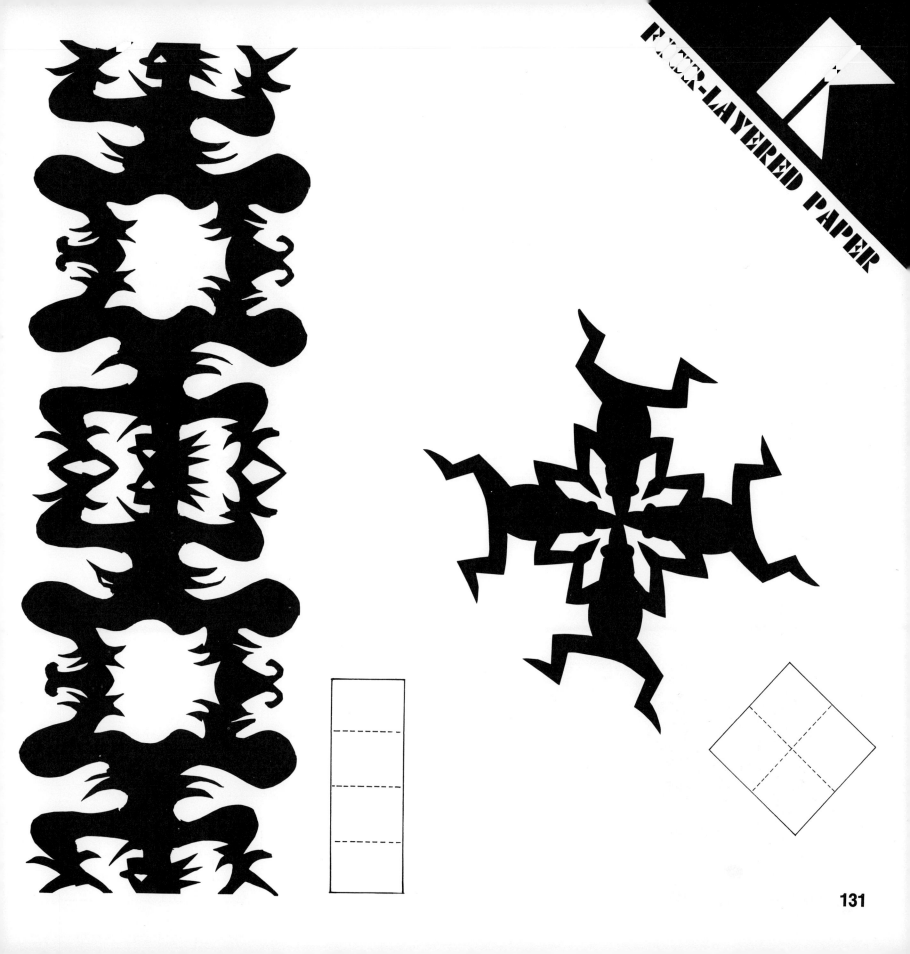

PAPER IS FOLDED
ON THE DIAGONAL.

This eight-layered fold is
the most versatile basis
for paper cutting.

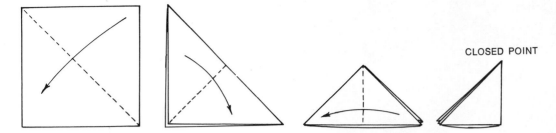

CLOSED POINT

round

Round doilies and other
designs are made by first
making a curved cut.

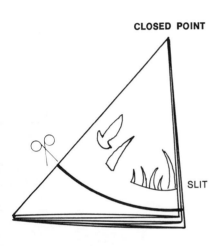

CLOSED POINT

SLIT

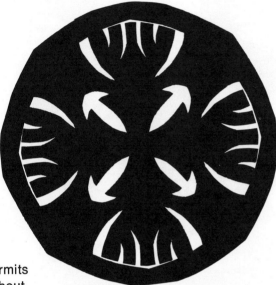

Note slit which permits
interior cutting without
piercing a hole first. This
method is based on the
Mexican bark paper
cut-out shown below.

When cutting on multi-
layered paper it is
important to bear in
mind that the folded
edges keep the designs
together. Parts of the
folded edges may be cut
away, but any cut from
one edge to another will
cause the design to fall
apart. With circular cut-
outs, keep in mind which
corner is the center of
the design.

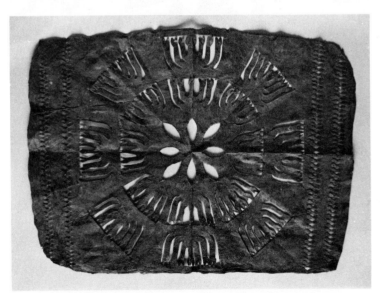

basket

Parallel cuts are made from folded edge. Then from open edge, slits are made in between. Design has to be unfolded very carefully, reversing the prefolding steps. To suspend, reinforce center with small cardboard square and then thread. This basket is a variation of the stretch paper technique.

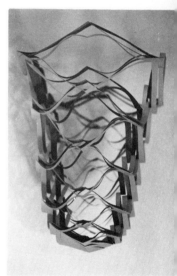

CLOSED POINT

FOLDED EDGE

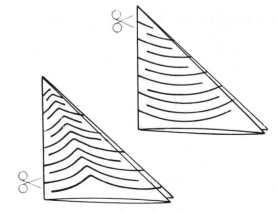

decoration

Staple two baskets together at the four corners to make a Christmas decoration.

133

stars

Stars are fascinating and they are symbolic in many cultures. This is reflected in the national flags of different countries. Legend has it that Betsy Ross, the creator of the American flag, presented a star puzzle to George Washington. The challenge was to fold a piece of paper in such a way that it would produce a five-pointed star with a single cut. We do not know whether he was able to solve the puzzle, but it is easy to cut stars with varying numbers of points once you know how to prefold the paper.

I am most frequently asked to demonstrate the five-pointed star, either because people have seen it made previously or because they themselves were able to make it at one time, but have forgotten the method. An interesting point to remember when making stars is that the angle of the points can be changed easily. For example, a star can be very shallow or quite spiky, depending on the angle of the cut. Before cutting into that one sheet of paper you may have reserved for a dramatic Christmas decoration, experiment with newspaper. Voice of experience speaking!

Stars can be used in many decorative ways. Four- and eight-pointed ones will give a restful feeling, whereas the five-pointed star is attention getting.

To make stars from cardboard or paper too thick to prefold, first cut a pattern from lightweight paper and trace the outline onto the cardboard.

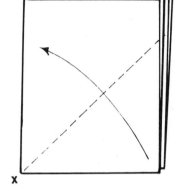

x

Fold as shown by dotted line. Be sure fold goes through center point of paper, X.

Cut on heavy line. Unfold.

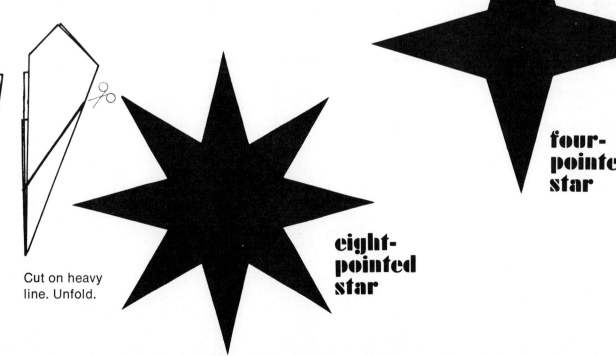

four-pointed star

eight-pointed star

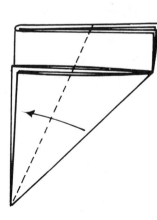

Prefold paper as for four-pointed star. Fold on dotted line.

Cut on heavy line. Unfold.

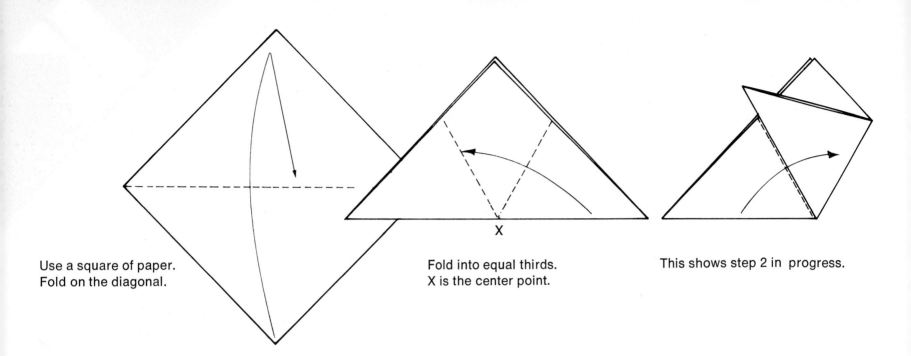

Use a square of paper.
Fold on the diagonal.

Fold into equal thirds.
X is the center point.

This shows step 2 in progress.

A five-pointed star needs only one cut, but the prefolding is quite tricky.

Use a piece of paper
8″ x 10″ [20 cm x 25 cm].
Fold in half the short
way.

Fold top edge to bottom
edge and make a small
crease to indicate
half-way mark.

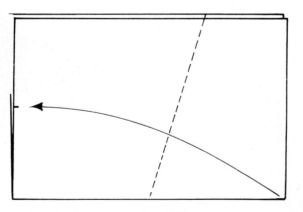

Bring right corner to the half-way
mark you made on opposite edge,
and crease as shown by dotted line.

Fold right edge over to
left and crease as shown
by dotted line.

Now fold left edge
over to right and
crease as shown
by dotted line.

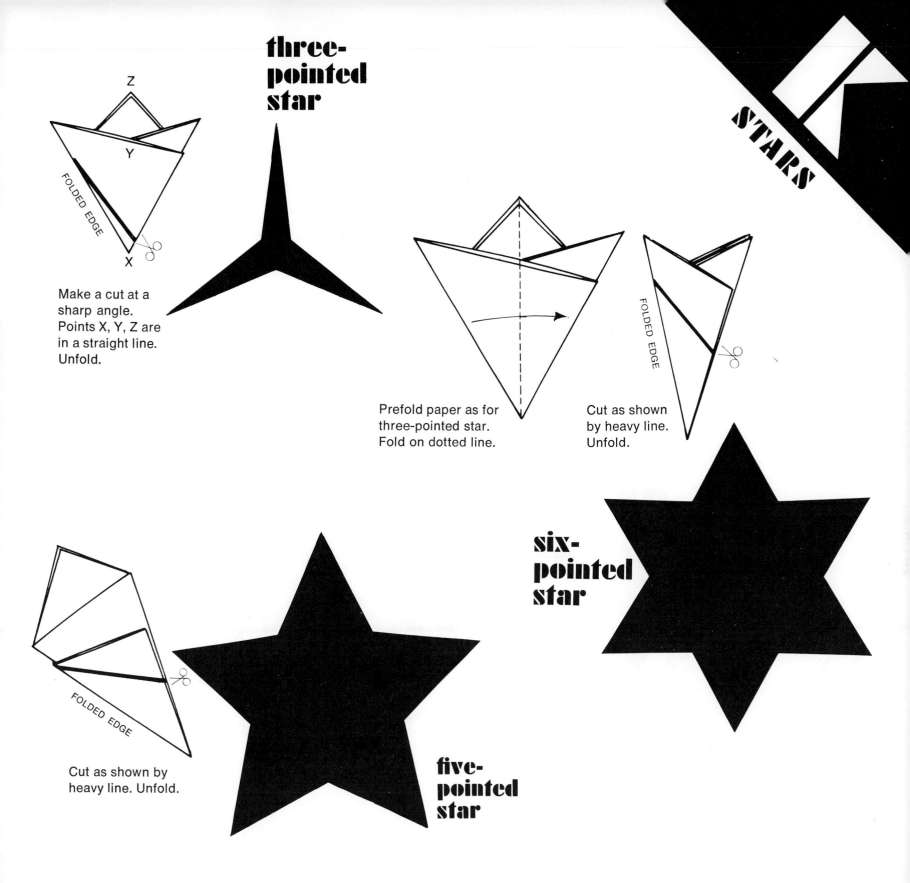

three-pointed star

Make a cut at a sharp angle. Points X, Y, Z are in a straight line. Unfold.

Prefold paper as for three-pointed star. Fold on dotted line.

Cut as shown by heavy line. Unfold.

six-pointed star

five-pointed star

Cut as shown by heavy line. Unfold.

pierced stars

See Four-Pointed Star

See Eight-Pointed Star

star variations

Star patterns are the basis for many interesting designs. Some possibilities are shown here, with cutting patterns. The ideas shown are interchangeable. For example, any prefold for a star can be cut as a pierced star. Any of the other ideas, as well as many of the cutting techniques illustrated throughout the book, can be applied with success to the various star folds. Small cut-outs or parallel cuts will add light and dark contrasts. Pieces that fall off in cutting can be used for greeting card designs and other collages.

Attractive three-dimensional decorations are made by gathering the points of stars together. On an Eight-Pointed Star, alternate points can be gathered, leaving four to reach outward. Merely mountain or valley folding the points can produce different results and experimenting with this and other variables will result in rounded or pear-shaped ornaments for making mobiles.

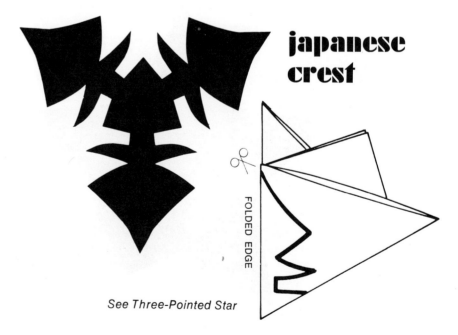

japanese crest

See Three-Pointed Star

See Six-Pointed Star

FOLDED EDGE

snowflake

flower

hexagon

FOLDED EDGE

See Six-Pointed Star

FOLDED EDGE

See Five-Pointed Star

141

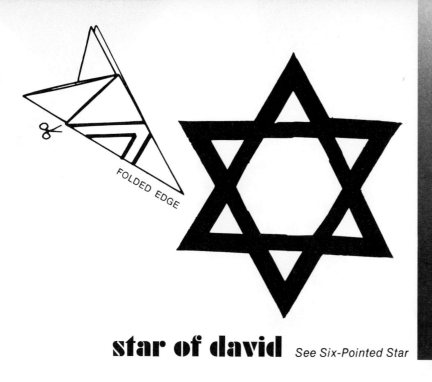

star of david *See Six-Pointed Star*

FOLDED EDGE

star of bethlehem

See Four-Pointed Star

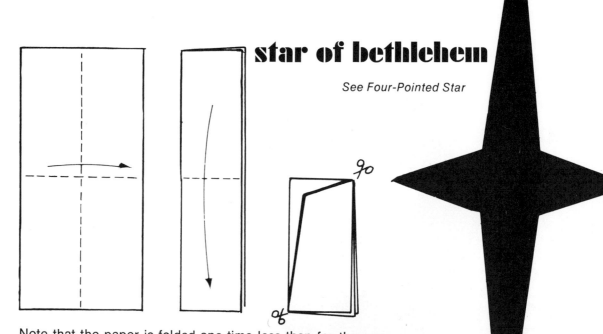

Note that the paper is folded one time less than for the regular Four-Pointed Star. Eight- and Ten-Pointed Stars can be made by the same method on different prefolds.

how to make stars three-dimensional

Fold up on short dimension, making valley fold.

Fold down from point to point, making mountain fold.

Paper can be woven, using actual textile methods. This weave is made from two pieces of strong paper.

Take two same size pieces of contrasting paper.

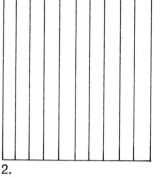

1.
Fold first piece in half, cut parallel. Unfold.

2.
Cut second piece into strips.

This variation is made from strips of paper, which have been doubled over lengthwise to add strength. Step pattern is produced by passing over and under two strands at a time.

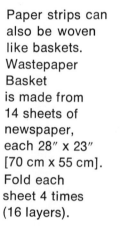

Other variations are changing the width of the strips, using patterned paper, cutting the strips in waves or at angles. Experimentation will quickly suggest other interesting combinations. Woven paper can be utilized for placemats or wall decorations.

Paper strips can also be woven like baskets. Wastepaper Basket is made from 14 sheets of newspaper, each 28″ x 23″ [70 cm x 55 cm]. Fold each sheet 4 times (16 layers).

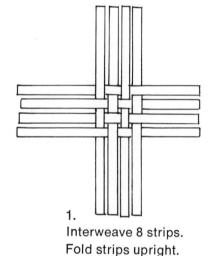

1.
Interweave 8 strips. Fold strips upright.

This shows a reed pattern made into a three-dimensional border by winding two strips around a center strip, always at forty-five degrees. A fairly substantial bracelet can be made in this way. Use silver paper, 10″ x 1½″ [25 x 4 cm] for the center strip and two gold paper strips, 15″ x 1″ [40 cm x 2½ cm]. All three strips are first folded in half lengthwise.

After trimming and pasting down the ends, the bracelet is 8¾″ [22 cm] long. A neat closure is made by sliding the ends into each other.

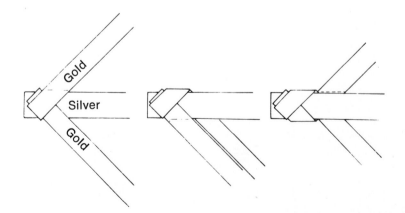

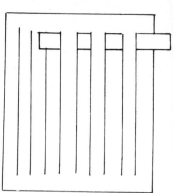

mat

3.
Weave strips into the
first piece of paper.

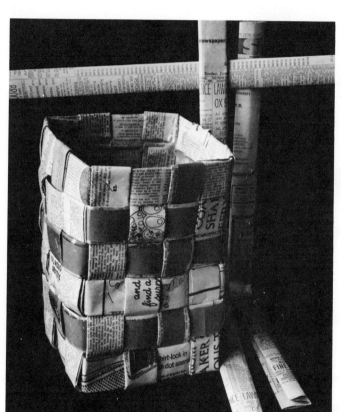

2.
Weave remaining six strips around.
Staple, glue or cellophane tape
as necessary.

**waste
paper
basket**

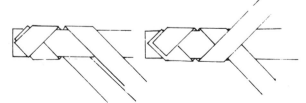

bracelet

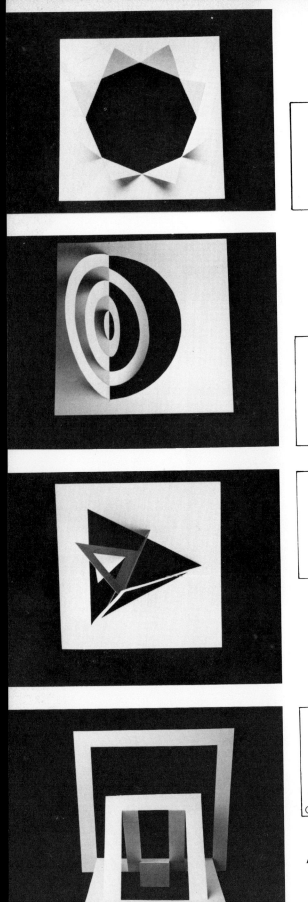

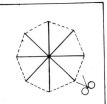

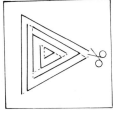

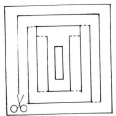

After cutting, mountain and valley fold on dotted lines.

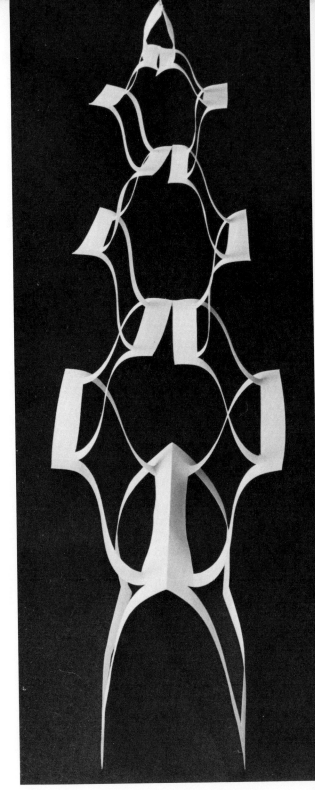

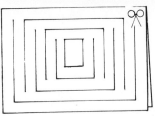

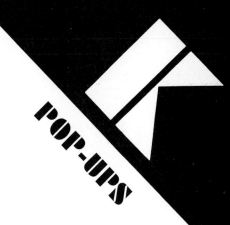

Three-dimensional cards are made by combining folding and cutting.

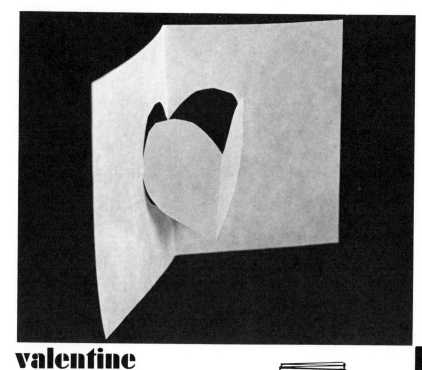

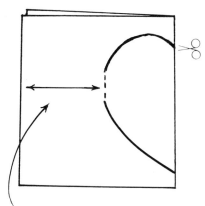

This dimension has to be longer than the portion used for the cut-out.

valentine

christmas card

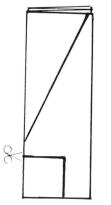

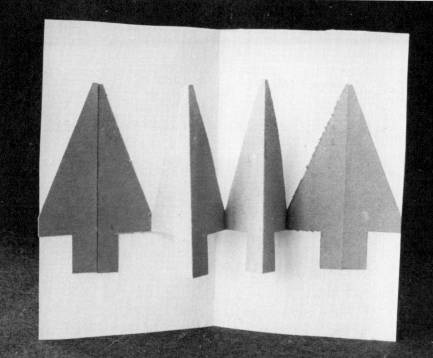

Another idea is to glue an accordion pleated piece of paper to the inside of a greeting card. When the card is opened, the pleated paper expands. This paper inset may be precut in different shapes. Here it is cut as a tree. These cards may be enhanced by applying different cuts, folds and decorations.

CUTTING CHART

The purpose of the chart is to spur your imagination.
Read vertical column for paper preparation.
Read horizontal column for cutting techniques.
Each square represents a possible combination.

Fold in any of the ways and apply any cutting procedure.
The squares which are filled in are variations
shown in the book.
The empty spaces are for your own designs.

cutting procedure

paper preparation	PARALLEL CUTS	GEOMETRIC CUTS	EDGE CUTTING	SILHOUETTE	INTERIOR CUTTING	SPIRAL
FLAT	sliced egg p. 123			cat p. 125	panda p. 124	
FOLDED ONCE	wall decoration p. 126		pop-up p. 147	bird p. 127	fertility figure p. 127	
PLEATED		chains p. 129		paper dolls p. 128		
FOUR-LAYERED		four-pointed star p. 137		frogs p. 131		mobile p. 130
EIGHT-LAYERED	basket p. 133		doily p. 132			
OTHER PREFOLDS		butterfly p. 135	snowflake p. 134			

This section, which I call Composites, brings together ideas for combining paper cuts with each other.

DISCARDS.   A by-product of paper-cutting is the paper that falls away and necessitates a good clean-up when one is finished, but these paper snips often have attractive forms and can be used on their own. For example, the petal-shaped pieces cut away from the Eight-Pointed Star variation (page 140) can be arranged in a circle or overlapped in a repetitive border.

POSITIVE AND NEGATIVE SPACE RELATIONS.
This mask illustrates that the areas which are cut away, negative space, can be as important as the main ground, positive space.

COLLAGE.   Paper is well suited to collage, the art of arranging shapes of different colors and textures. All types of paper can be used, but magazine pages are a favorite source of mine because of their subtle color combinations and various densities of print. Overlapping tissue paper provides varying color values and intensity. Books on collage or design are available for additional information. See Bibliography on page 189.

Here are a few more suggestions for combining techniques previously shown.

DANCING DOLL.   Cut out a paper doll from lightweight paper, folded once. Make alternating parallel cuts. Stretch paper by holding the doll by the head and the feet. Then hold the doll at the top and bounce it up and down. It seems to be jumping and dancing.

HUMAN FIGURES.   Cut out the body, head and limbs separately and assemble them on background paper. It is easier to make running figures this way than to cut them out in one piece. The separate parts can be rearranged before final pasting.

TRANSLUCENT PAPER.   Place two pieces of paper together. Perforate them with a paper punch or cut out small areas. Glue a piece of colored tissue paper between the two layers of perforated paper. Hang it up against a light or attach to a window.

COMBINING MATERIALS.   Paper cut-outs can be decorated with felt pens, buttons and other natural or man-made materials. Cut-outs themselves can be applied to paper goods, wall decorations and furniture.

PAPER SCULPTED

SCULPTURE

fold here

fold here

Paper Constructions by students,
University of Washington.
Photograph courtesy, Pauline
Johnson

PAPER · SCULPTED

background

Traditional Portuguese "Palmito," for religious procession and decoration made from metallic paper. Leaf veins are pressed over knitting needles.

Paper Bas-Relief Sculpture,
by Ray Ameijide, American

INTRODUCTION

I define paper sculpture as a three-dimensional assemblage made from paper and held in position by auxiliary materials, such as glue or staples. To demonstrate a simple paper sculpture, take a strip of paper, twist it and staple the two ends together.

Sculpture is most easily visualized as freestanding, but paper lends itself well to bas relief, a picture in which the design projects from the background. Both of these kinds of sculpture can be made either from one piece of paper or a combination of various shapes which are already folded. The light effects play an important role in paper sculpture as is easily demonstrated on a pleated piece of white paper. Although the color of the paper is the same throughout, some portions appear darker than others depending on the position of the light source. White paper is traditionally used to take full advantage of light contrast, but nowadays some artists use color to achieve individual objectives.

The relatively few basic techniques have to be combined with imagination to achieve satisfactory sculptures. Studying the work of established artists will give you ideas of what can be done, and for this reason this section includes a number of photographs of their work.

The term paper sculpture is fairly recent in historical perspective, although variations of paper cutting techniques practiced in different countries can be considered a kind of paper sculpture. The Portuguese *palmito,* a paper floral spray carried in religious processions, is an elaborate example originating from a country without a strong paper craft tradition. Chinese burial papers are an important category, described in greater detail on page 19.

Modern paper sculpture received its greatest impetus from the Bauhaus in the 1920's. In the 1930's a stylized realism originated in Poland and reached its highest point of development in England. At one time paper sculptures appeared frequently as store window displays and at present the Goldsmith's College School of Art in London includes a regular course on this subject. This style is illustrated here by the work of Ray Ameijide, an American artist.

Many art and architecture schools all over the world now include paper sculpture in their curriculum and their graduates have applied the designs to advertising and show window displays. Scandinavian interest in three-dimensional paper craft can be seen in the Danish and Swedish paper ornaments which are available in many countries.

Looking ahead, I think paper sculpture will become more and more popular for interior decoration, as it offers an inexpensive way to experiment in an era of change.

155

materials

Any stiff paper is suitable for paper sculpture. Two-ply Bristol board is good for general purposes and usually available in art stores.

Deckled papers give a textured effect.

Thin cardboard is required for larger structures.

Paper grain is the direction taken by a majority of the fibers in any sheet of paper. Paper rolls more easily with the grain.

Grain may interfere with the way you wish to bend or roll the paper and it will help to "break" the grain by pulling it firmly over the edge of a table or between a metal ruler and a table top.

In a cylinder the grain direction must be vertical for greatest strength.

Paper will tear more cleanly in the direction of the grain.

tools

Scissors
X-Acto knife or kitchen knife
Ruler (metal or with a metal edge)
Magazines, used as a base for cutting and for protecting the table surface
Pencil
Compass (with pencil or double points)
Glue (Elmer's or Sobo)
Rubber cement
Paper clips
Straight pins
Cellophane tape
Stapler

Additional Useful Tools
Spring clothespins
Triangle
T-square
Double-pronged brass brads
Double-faced cellophane tape
French curve

basic shapes

Separate shapes can be combined to make a sculpture.

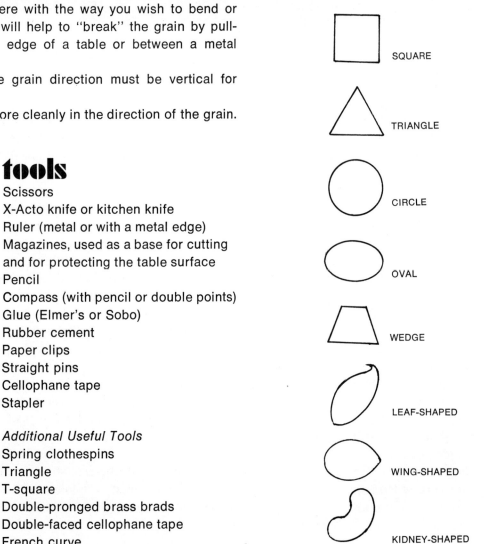

RECTANGLE

SQUARE

TRIANGLE

CIRCLE

OVAL

WEDGE

LEAF-SHAPED

WING-SHAPED

KIDNEY-SHAPED

Paper Sculpture, by Benigna Chilla. Photograph Clemens Kalischer

Angel Sculpture, by Paul Lobel, "Paperteer," American jeweller, who became a paper sculptor through making paper mock-ups for brooches and other pieces.

graphic symbols

VALLEY FOLD _

MOUNTAIN FOLD _ _.._ _ _ _.._ _ _ _ _.._ _ _ _ _.._ _ _

CUT—heavy line and scissors ━━━━━━━━━✄

procedures

helpful cutting hints

ALL KNIFE CUTTING MUST BE DONE ON A PROTECTED SURFACE.   Wooden, masonite or plastic boards are best, but cardboard, glass or magazines may be used as the underlay.

The basic shapes are cut out with an X-Acto knife which gives a clean cut, although scissors may be used. It does not take long to get used to working with a knife. To cut straight lines, guide the knife along the edge of a ruler in several short strokes, rather than one continuous line, exerting a little extra pressure at the beginning and the end of paper.

creative experiment

Before turning the page, cut out circles, triangles and other shapes from heavy paper and manipulate them into three-dimensional forms in any way you wish. Practice making smooth cuts.

rolling

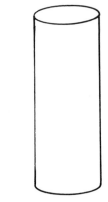

Rectangle rolled
into a cylinder.

lampshade

A wedge is rolled
into a cone.

witch's hat

decoration

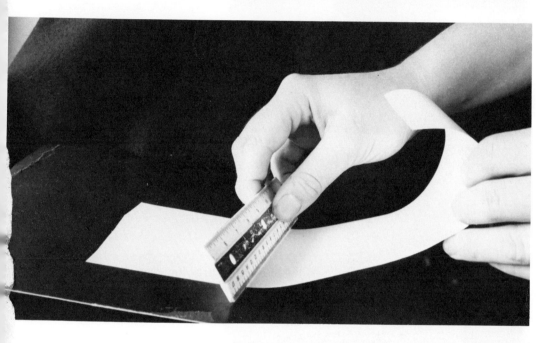

bending

A strip is bent by
drawing ruler alternately
against front and then the
back of the paper.

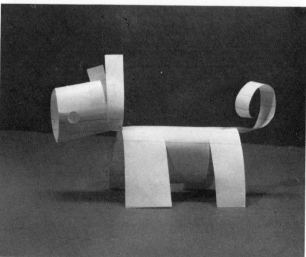

dog

snake

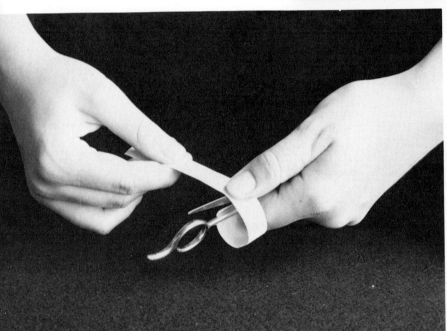

Strips of paper can be curled by drawing over the cutting edge of the scissors. Curling is useful for simulating hair, flower petals, pine needles or other patterns occurring in nature.

flower

162

Sculpture, scored, folded and glued,
8" x 4", by Hiroshi Ogawa, Japanese.
Photograph: Courtesy, The Museum of
Contemporary Crafts, New York.

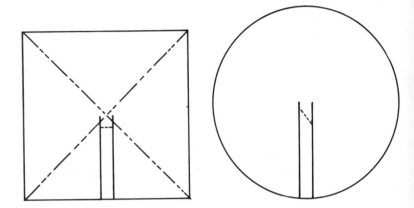

checkers

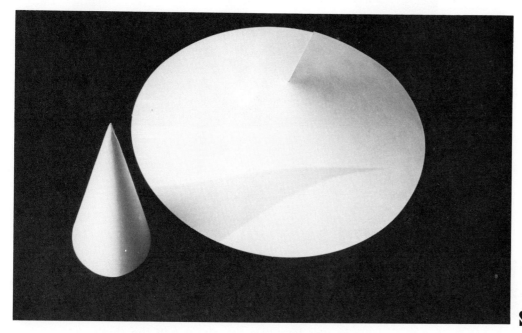

sun hat

fish   pinwheel   shield

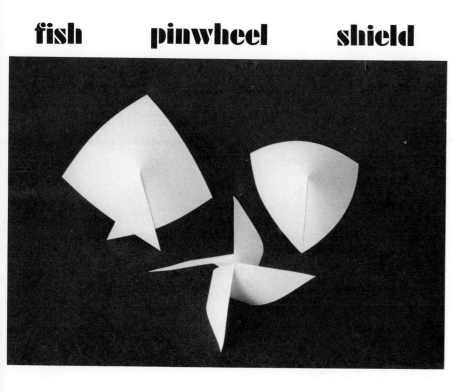

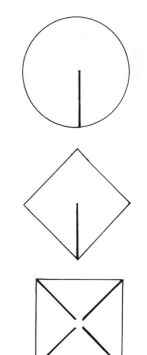

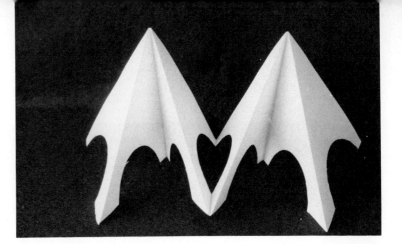

scoring

The most characteristic technique of paper sculpture is the Score, which permits stiff paper and cardboard to be folded in clean, sharp lines. Straight scoring is done by guiding the point of the scissors or X-Acto knife along a ruler's metal edge, scratching the line through about half the thickness of the paper. Care must be taken not to cut all the way through, but you will soon find just the right amount of pressure needed.

Experiment by scoring a straight line on a file card or similar paper. Compare this with an unscored fold line, which will appear rough.

Folding emphasizes the contrasting effects of light.
    Accordion pleats are made by scoring lines alternately on the front and the back of the paper.

Dotted lines are scored on the front of the paper.
Dot-dash lines on the back.

PAPER IS ALWAYS FOLDED AWAY FROM THE SCORE

The scored curve is surprisingly easy to execute and adds a graceful quality to the work.
    Curved lines can be scored freehand, along a circular object such as a plate or a can, or along a French curve. A double-pointed compass is also helpful.
    Smoother lines can be made by moving the paper and holding the knife still.

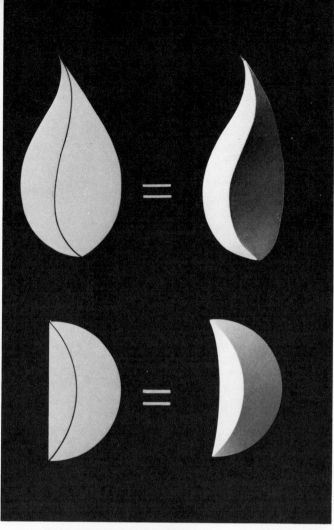

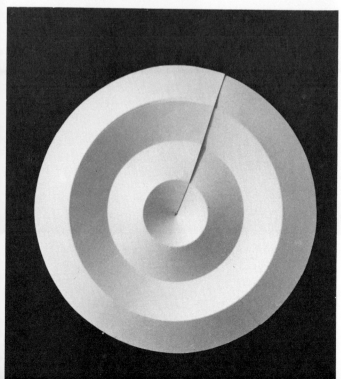

FOLD ON THE SCORED LINES,
AWAY FROM THE INCISION.

curved lines
leaf

Score the center vein on
one side of the paper.

CIRCULAR SHAPES can
also be scored
alternately on the front
and the back on lines
through the center,

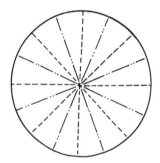

or concentrically.

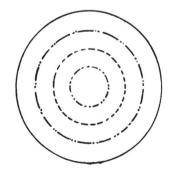

straight lines

167

graphic

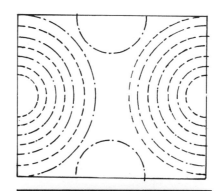

ornaments

owl

The cuts on the Owl were done freehand, but precise patterns have to be measured and drawn in with a soft pencil before cutting. This technique adds a great deal of light-and-dark contrast.

Folding and cutting procedures shown previously can be applied.

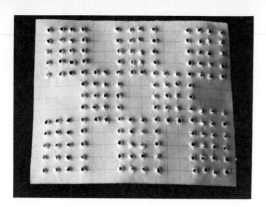

Texture can be added to sculpture surfaces by cutting, hole punching, adding small folded or cut pieces of paper, weaving strips of paper in and out.

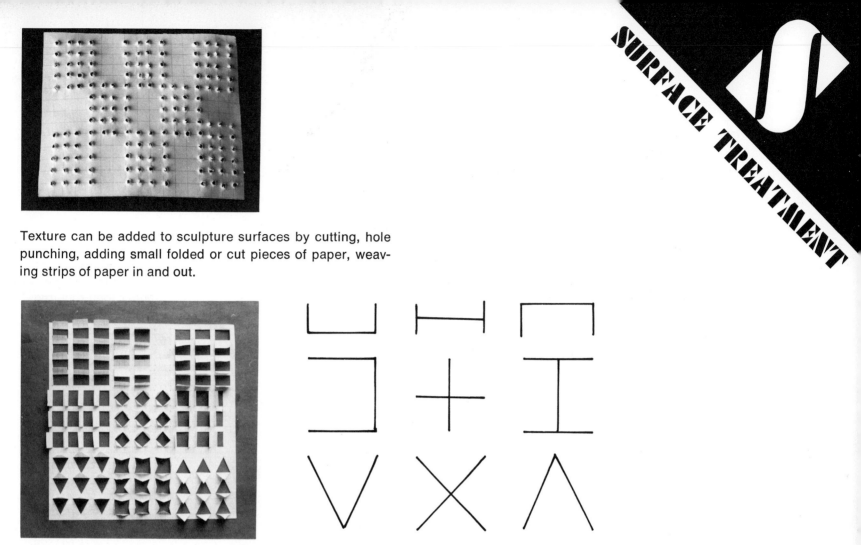

Here are some straight cuts which give interesting surface texture when multiplied and applied in overall patterns.

Other effects can be achieved on pleated paper.

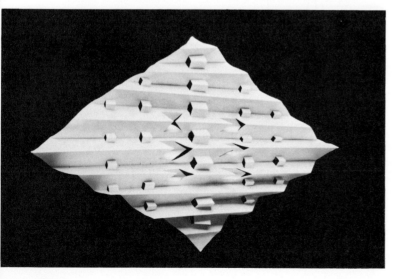

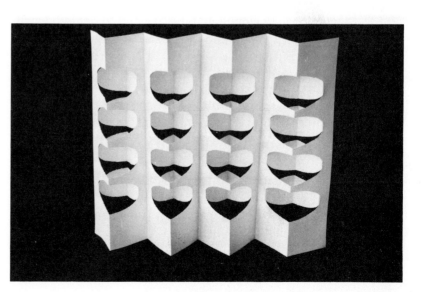

171

To maintain a basic shape in three-dimensional form, fastening is necessary.

PASTING *White glue* Various suitable brands are available but I have found Sobo to be the most satisfactory.

Rubber cement This is a transparent rubbery substance, obtainable in stationery stores, and should not be confused with cement used to repair rubber articles, such as tires. It can be used as a temporary or permanent bond, depending on the way it is applied.
TEMPORARY BOND: To bind two edges together, apply rubber cement to *one* surface only, then press the edges together. Later they can easily be separated without damage to the paper. This is very useful for experimenting with the exact position desired. Excess cement can be rubbed off with the fingers.
PERMANENT BOND: Rubber cement can be made into a permanent bond by applying it to both edges, letting it get almost dry and then pressing the edges together. Although unexcelled as a temporary bond rubber cement may discolor some papers after a period of time.

Cellophane tape Very easy to use in its various forms: *Regular, Magic* (Matte), which is hardly noticeable, and *Double-faced.*
Cellophane tape may discolor and become brittle after a period of time.

STAPLES Stapling is very simple, but it is difficult to get into small openings. The metal line of the staple may detract from the purity of the design, except in hidden spots and on temporary decorations.
Staplers with 12″ arms are available.

STRAIGHT PINS Can be used for temporary or permanent fastening. Care must be taken in handling the sculpture, particularly by children.

DOUBLE-PRONGED BRADS Useful for the joints of movable figures.

TEMPORARY FASTENING Paper clips and spring clothespins are useful aids for holding joinings in place.

tabs

Tabs are small flaps that extend from the edge of the basic shape.
First cut tab on edge A. Lay it on edge B. Mark with pencil. Slit with knife.

A tube is attached to a base as follows: Cut tube longer than required. Cut extra length into tabs. Spread tabs apart and glue them to the base.

hinges

Hinges are made of small strips of tape.

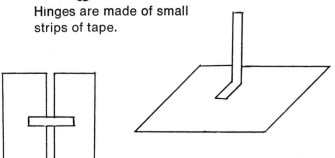

interior tabs

Tabs can be cut as part of a design, and this method is illustrated by a round mobile, where the v-shaped cut acts as a hinge.

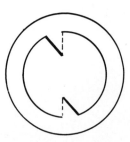

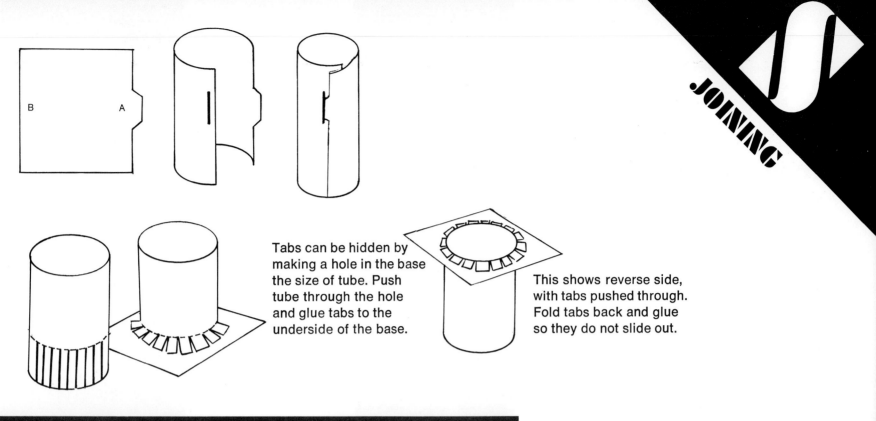

Tabs can be hidden by making a hole in the base the size of tube. Push tube through the hole and glue tabs to the underside of the base.

This shows reverse side, with tabs pushed through. Fold tabs back and glue so they do not slide out.

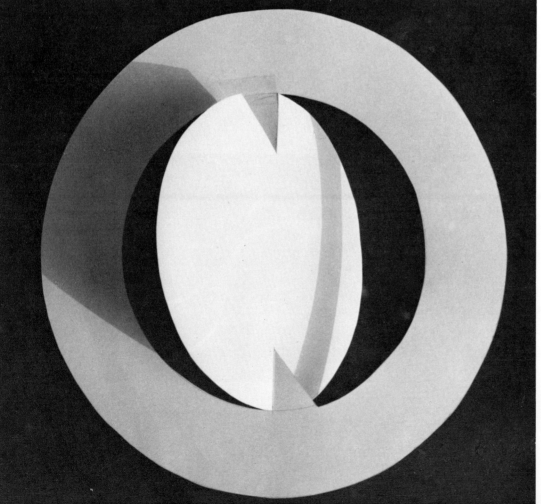

mobile

interlocking slits

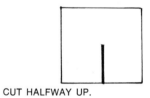

CUT HALFWAY UP.

CUT HALFWAY DOWN.

SLIDE INTO EACH OTHER.

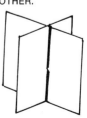

Varying lengths of paper strips
can be combined and
brought together at intervals.

triple circle

Here three different length
strips are shaped into
circles and stapled together.

looped circle

one strip, 1″ x 30″ [2 cm x 75 cm]
one strip, 1″ x 10″ [2 cm x 25 cm]
Loops are made by stapling
long strip to short strip
at 1¾″ [4 cm] intervals.
This is made into a circle by
stapling overlap together.

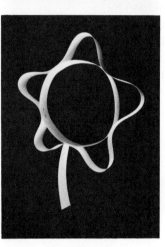

bird

Two strips ¾″ x 9″ [2 cm x 22 cm], cut wider at one end.

Cut wide ends into strips for tail. Staple strips together at
both ends but leave tail feathers free. Staple once more
about 1″ [2½ cm] from the beak, manipulating strips until
they form a small loop for the head and a larger loop for
the body.

Curl tail strips over scissor edge.

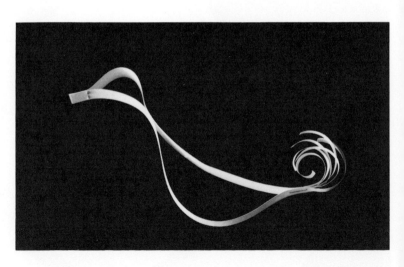

174

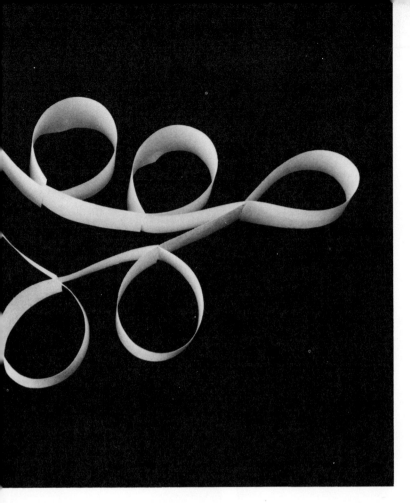

heart

This decoration is made from ½″ [1 cm] wide strips:
three strips 9″ long,
two strips 7½″ long and
two strips 6″ long.

First they are stapled together.

Then three strips on each side are pulled down and stapled again.

Center strip is hanger.

175

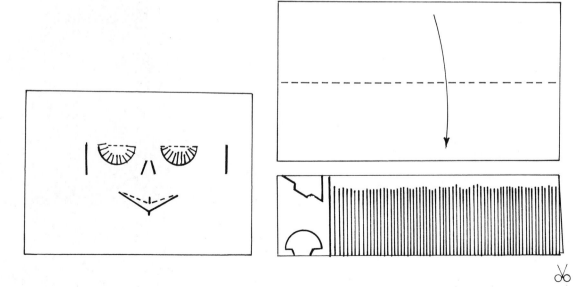

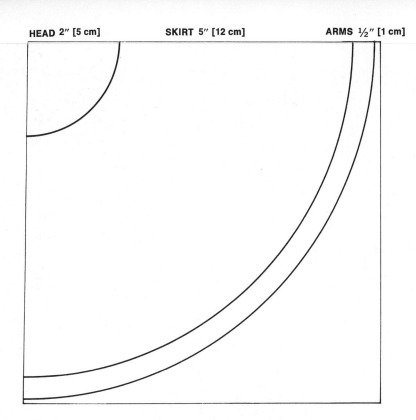

HEAD 2″ [5 cm]   SKIRT 5″ [12 cm]   ARMS ½″ [1 cm]

Roll head and skirt into cones and fasten. Snip off top corner of skirt and insert pointed end of head cone. Secure with cellophane tape. Paste on arms which may be narrowed to taste. Doll can assume different positions by varying angle of head. Bottom edge of skirt can be shortened in front or back to balance figure in other poses.

cone doll

face

Use two sheets 8½″ x 11″ [21 cm x 29 cm].
Cut eyes and mouth on heavy lines. Fold on dotted lines.
Cut slots for ears and nose.
Cut out nose and tab.
Cut and curl hair.
Cut two ears from doubled piece of paper.

To assemble:
Staple or tape hair to top of face. Roll paper into cylinder and staple. Insert tabs of ears and nose into slots.

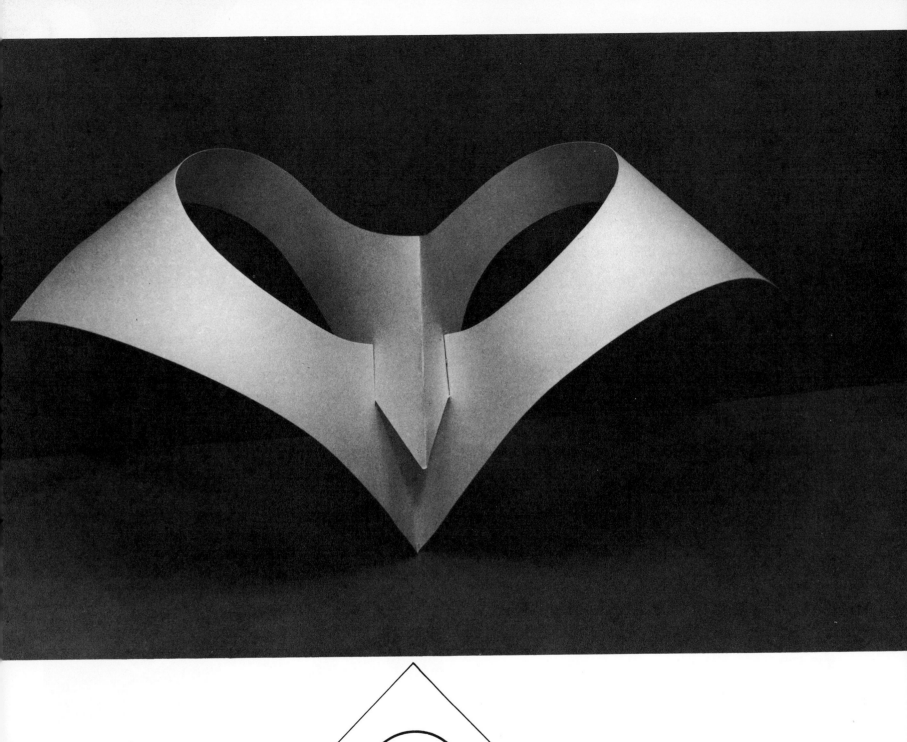

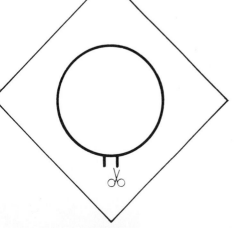

geometric models

Following are patterns for making a pyramid and a cube. Other geometric solids can be made in this fashion and be used as graphic demonstrations in the mathematics class, as well as for pedestal stands and suspended decorations.

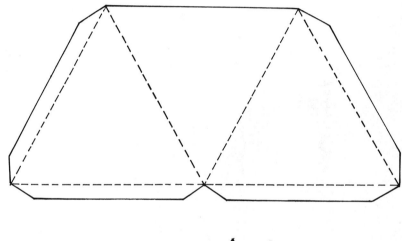

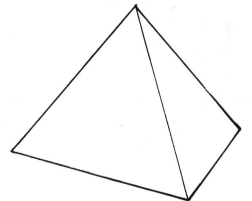

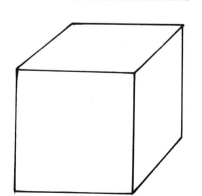

reinforcing supports

There are various methods of giving stability to paper sculptures. Cardboard tubes and cones are usually sufficient, but larger sculptures may require armatures of light wood or wire.

Spatial structure, scored and
folded paper strips, 25″ cube.
Student project directed by Kurt
Londenberg, Hamburg, Germany.

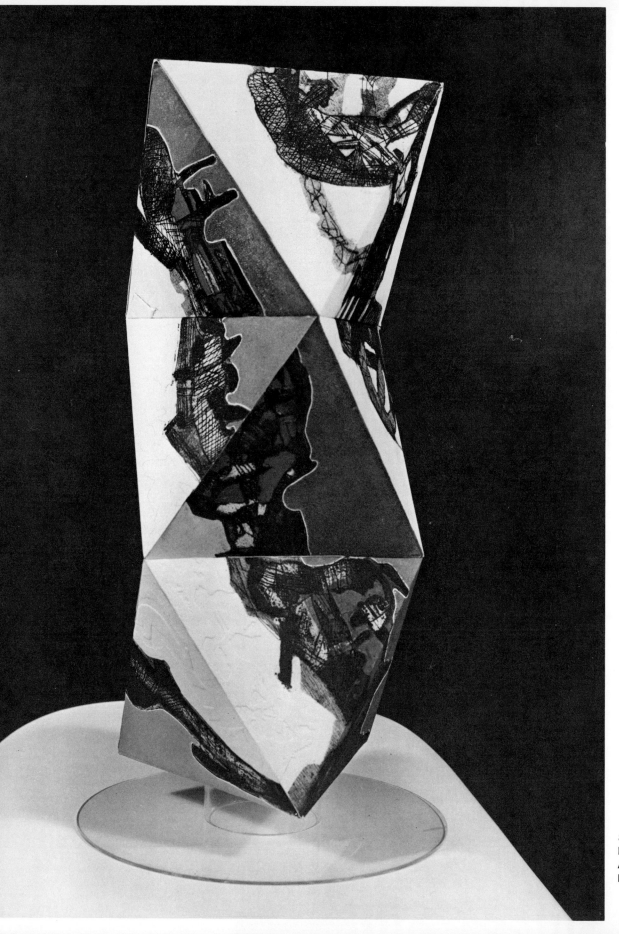

APPENDIX

Spiral, three-color folded intaglio,
by Juan Gomez Quiroz. Courtesy
Alonza Gallery, New York.
Photograph Bill Freeman.

Multicolor Bas-Relief Sculpture,
by Dr. Emanuel Mooser, Swiss.

Sculpture made from red, blue
and yellow paper strips by
Dr. Emanuel Mooser.

instant color help

Color is an intrinsic part of paper craft and choice of color is especially important when several components are involved in a paper sculpture, a mobile, a paper flower arrangement or decorations for a party.

Color theories described in books on decorating, painting, optics or psychology can be applied to paper construction, but I have found that the following simple color schemes always work well:

1. Use different values of one color, such as

light blue		pale gray
medium blue	or	medium gray
dark blue.		black.

2. Use a color wheel and select
   two adjacent colors or
   two opposite colors.
3. To any of these colors add white or black, or both.
4. Select color combinations from fabrics, wallpapers, gift-wrap papers and advertisements. They were designed by competent artists and you can benefit from their experience.

Although these are basic principles, good design involves certain relationships and proportions which an experienced designer has learned to handle. The flexibility and low cost of paper make it easy to experiment and place colors in many variations until a color scheme looks right. Have faith in your own judgment, as your feeling expresses your personality and is probably based on the experience gained unconsciously over the years. The more you work with color, the more your understanding and competence will increase.

how to entertain

After you have become proficient in paper craft and your friends have enjoyed watching you, you may want to use your talent publicly. The occasion may be a class assignment or a business presentation, or you may be asked to present a program in a classroom or at a local club. Here are a few hints that may be helpful.

First choose designs appropriate to your particular purpose, the season of the year and the interest of the group. Then make absolutely sure that you know the patterns well by going over them step by step. Use large pieces of paper that can be seen easily from the back of the room.

For a complete program, decide on the historical and other background information you wish to include in your talk. Most people enjoy hearing about your personal experiences with paper—how delighted you were when you were first able to make something, how it helped to pass a tense moment for an anxious child, or any lighthearted anecdote. The audience is always on your side and interested in what you have to say, but if you are nervous, pretend you are talking to a friend, a trick which novice speakers find very relaxing. In addition the paper is a prop that helps you hold audience attention. I have found that favorites are the Flapping Bird (page 83), the House Fold (page 53) changed into several different things, and such a sequence based on the Multiform (page 56).

Besides demonstrating, you may wish to teach how to make one or two things. Audience participation is always more fun and both paper folding and paper cutting are effective. For origami, only paper is required, but for cutting you must also provide scissors. Make doubly sure that you know how to make each model. To prepare yourself for teaching, practice making the model many times while reading the step-by-step instructions out loud to yourself. Choose simple models and do not teach too many things in one session, as this may be confusing. In a school the complexity of the models must be suitable to the grade level.

If you intend to teach, find out how many will attend your demonstration so that you can prepare the right amount of paper. In a classroom the number can usually be anticipated very closely and a club can estimate based on past attendance. Always bring more paper than you think you can possibly need. You must also make up your mind on the format of your presentation, which may be governed by the room arrangement. Your choice is between a lecture demonstration or a workshop. The latter is only suitable for small groups. Here is a checklist of items to be assembled in a carton, preferably covered with colorful paper and decorated with paper craft.

A list of models you will demonstrate and those you will teach, in order of performance. This will serve as a prompter during your presentation.

Extra large pieces of paper for yourself, that are easy to see, between 10″ [25 cm] and 15″ [37.5 cm].

Any exhibition models, preferably large, and books which you may wish to display.

Paper for the audience, if they are to work along with you. Colored typewriter paper is most convenient to prepare.

Scissors, if you intend to teach paper cutting.

And now good luck with your program!

Origami Demonstration in a Garden. Photograph Ralph Grant.

TO THE TEACHER

Children enjoy paper craft and this appeal can be turned to good advantage in furthering educational goals.

You will find that many of the general suggestions made under How to Use the Paper Craft Designs in the introductory section of the book are adaptable to the classroom. Here are some more ideas.

For the art class

Ask students to bring in all kinds of paper—notebook pages, bus tickets, magazines, newspaper, shopping bags, wax paper, facial tissue, etc. Ask them to feel the texture and verbalize their sensations—smooth, rough, hairy, slippery, feels like a dried leaf, springy, crisp, won't hold a crease. This exercise heightens tactile awareness.

Ask students to cut free-form shapes and arrange them in a collage.

Challenge the students to use every part of a sheet of paper to make a design without discarding anything. Paper may be cut, glued, etc.

Provide paper in two colors to be combined in an assemblage.

Have students cut a small and a large square in three colors. Ask them to describe the size of the squares as they appear in different combinations.

Ask students to design signs that convey a message at a glance. Examples are an arrow for a road sign; a bicycle for a bicycle parking area; an animal for an animal hospital.

Ask students to create three-dimensional designs from flat paper using fastening aids.

Ask students to create simple abstract or realistic designs from squares and rectangles, by folding only. This introduces students to the principles of origami.

Add surface texture to a piece of paper to suggest hair, grass, doors, etc. by cutting slits, adding bits of paper, pin-pricking and other means.

Fold tissue paper and tie dye it.

Provide strips of paper for strip figures and objects.

Demonstrate a cutting or folding procedure described in this book and ask students to experiment with it. Depending on the technique, you can impose various limitations. For example, fold paper twice and make only one cut. This could be a continuous, curving cut all over the folded paper which would produce an elaborate design.

Encourage students to work on large-scale paper cuttings.

For the mathematics class

Let children cut out apples or any other shapes to demonstrate addition and subtraction.

Illustrate symmetry by making cuts on a folded piece of paper.

Demonstrate geometric concepts with paper. For example, a square cut in half makes two rectangles.

Have students cut angles. For example, the ninety-degree corner of a sheet of paper can be divided and the new angles measured.

Ask students to make simple origami models.

Ask students to construct the five platonic solids.

Challenge students to devise games and puzzles made from cut or folded paper. Many diversions in puzzle books can be illustrated this way.

Ask students to find out about Möbius' strip.

Teach students to make an origami model. Completely unfold it to the original square and ask students to analyze the geometric components of the pattern.

Other activities

Teachers have told me that they have integrated paper craft into many aspects of the curriculum. An example of a creative classroom exercise for social studies is to illustrate a unit with murals or three-dimensional mock-ups. A project in mask-making could lead to creative writing. Costumes and scenery can be made for school plays and dance recitals. Paper hats, necklaces, belts or scarves can be worn with leotards and jeans to indicate the characters. This calls for greater ingenuity than full costumes, but less investment in time and money. For oral reports or as an assignment in public speaking, have students take turns teaching other students to make a simple paper object. While the student-teacher is gaining valuable experience in presenting himself before a group, the class has the opportunity to observe processes of teaching and learning.

Objectives

To develop the sense for design and color.

To explore three-dimensional expression. Paper craft is a means of exploring three-dimensional space and may be particularly rewarding to children who have strong sculptural inclinations but are unable to draw well.

To increase co-ordination between the hand and the eye. More and more school systems are including paper craft in the curriculum, as educators recognize the importance of developing co-ordination through handcrafts.

To learn techniques. Techniques are the foundation of any craft. You can demonstrate a technique by teaching the class to make a specific object.

Following directions. In following your step-by-step directions for paper craft, children are learning to follow directions in general, a necessary ability.

To stimulate creativity and independent thought. The idea that everyone can create is fairly recent, but the creative spark must be encouraged. Allow students to use their imaginations and do not expect them to make identical things, unless you are teaching a technique or how to follow directions.

Some notes

I have presented programs on paper craft and particularly on origami in many schools, sometimes directly to the students and at other times to the teachers who took the ideas back to the classroom. Some of the teachers whom I met again from time to time were brimming with excitement when they recounted the unexpected results they had achieved from working with paper in this new way. Mainly they found that their classes loved to be involved with paper craft and that it provided a relaxed and friendly atmosphere.

Some students set to work right way to see what will happen, but others cannot think of what to make. Talking individually with hesitant students helps them come to a decision. Within a half-hour the crafters become very excited and talk to each other about their work and share the thrill of creating.

Paper work is also useful in occupying children who have completed a reading or other assignment, as they can busy themselves quietly and productively.

When a student has completed a project, it is a good idea to single out at least one feature for favorable comment which will reinforce pride in the work. It is not necessary that the work be perfect, but the student may be made aware that hard work and learned skills will improve his ability to produce things he likes to make.

Group projects.   Group work is a rewarding experience and should always be something that is too much for one child to accomplish by himself: a circus, an Indian village, a housing development, a space station, etc.

therapy

Paper craft is a successful tool in mental, physical and occupational therapy. It is particularly helpful in the following situations:

In sickness when patient is confined to bed.

In occupational therapy. It helps develop use of hands.

In mental therapy. Patient is able to complete an article in a short time, which gives him a feeling of accomplishment. At the same time it extends attention span and structures time.

Perceptual training.   Recent experimental studies by psychologists show that perceptual disabilities lead to learning difficulties and may affect behavior. Simple paper folding has been recommended as an exercise in hand and eye co-ordination to improve perceptual ability.

As a communications bridge.   Emotional tension may be relieved by talking to another person, but there are many other ways. A simple paper trick or origami may sometimes help establish rapport. A speech therapist who was having difficulty communicating with a disturbed patient attended one of my lectures. This gave her the idea of showing him an origami swan and indeed she was able to get a positive response for the first time. Since then she has taught herself about twenty-five simple origami figures which she uses in her practice with continuing success.

I have heard of other instances in group therapy where origami provided an atmosphere that permitted further interplay among the participants.

Art therapy. All these applications are in fact art therapy, which is a recently developed means of helping the emotionally and physically handicapped.

bibliography

This bibliography is confined to books which I consider standard. A comprehensive list of books on paper craft is available from:

> The Origami Center
> 71 West 11th Street
> New York, N.Y. 10011, U.S.A.

The list is revised every few months to include only books which are in print at the time and can be ordered from the Origami Center.

Information may also be obtained from:

> Mr. Michael Guy, The Secretary
> The British Origami Society
> 193 Abbey Road, Smethwick, Warley,
> Worcs. B67 5 NG, Great Britain

General paper craft

Johnson, Pauline. *Creating with Paper.* Seattle: University of Washington Press, 1958.
All aspects of handling paper explored. Profusely illustrated with photographs.

Paper folding

(All books are illustrated with how-to instructions.)

Brossman, Julia and Martin. *A Japanese Paper Folding Classic.* Washington, D.C.: Pinecone Press, 1961.
A scholarly book printed in a limited edition.

Gardner, Martin. *Second Scientific American Book of Puzzles and Diversions.* New York: Simon and Schuster, 1961.
Since 1957 Martin Gardner has been the contributor of a monthly column on mathematical recreations which appears in *Scientific American* magazine. He is the author of several books on the subject. One of his columns, devoted to origami, is included as chapter sixteen of this book. It illustrates mathematical aspects related to paper folding.

Harbin, Robert. *Origami, The Art of Paper Folding,* nos. 1, 2 and 3. Hodder Paperbacks, 1968, 1971, 1972.
Collection of folded paper models.

_____. *The Secrets of Origami.* London: Oldbourne Book Co., 1962.
A lively anthology of origami created by outstanding living artists. It includes such unusual folds as "The Moor on Horseback" by Adolfo Cercada. See also note about *The Best of Origami,* by Samuel Randlett.

Honda, Isao. *The World of Origami.* Tokyo: Japan Publications Trading Co., 1965.
Many animals.

Johnson, Donovan A. *Paper Folding for the Mathematics Class.* Washington, D.C.: National Council of Teachers of Mathematics, 1957.

Lewis, Shari and Oppenheimer, Lillian. *Folding Paper Puppets.* New York: Stein and Day, 1962.

_____. *Folding Paper Toys.* New York: Stein and Day, 1963.

_____. *Folding Paper Masks.* New York: Dutton, 1965.
Three books of simple origami for the beginner.

Randlett, Samuel. *The Best of Origami.* New York: Dutton, 1963.
An anthology of simple to advanced models by contemporary folders. It includes "Whistler's Mother in her Rocking Chair" by Fred Rohm. The author collaborated with Robert Harbin to avoid duplication with his *Secrets of Origami.*

Rottger, Ernst. *Creative Paper Design.* New York: Van Nostrand Reinhold, 1961.

Row, T. Sundara. *Geometric Exercises in Paper Folding.* New York: Dover Publications, 1966.
Strictly for those familiar with mathematics.

Sakoda, James. *Modern Origami.* New York: Simon and Schuster, 1969.
Fifty original folds by the author.

Temko, Florence and Simon, Elaine. *Paper Folding to Begin With.* Illustrated by Joan Stoliar. New York: Bobbs-Merrill, 1968.
Aimed at young children, but a colorful introduction to paper folding for all ages.

van Wisen, Betty. *Perceptual Training Activities Handbook.* New York: Teachers College Press, 1967.
Recommended for finding out how origami can be used in this special situation, but step-by-step directions are difficult to follow.

Yoshisawa, Akira. *Dokuhon (Creative Origami).* Tokyo: Kamakura Shobo Co., Ltd., 1969.
The finest of the master's works.

Paper cutting

Gardner, Martin. *New Mathematical Diversions from The Scientific American.* New York: Simon and Schuster, 1966.
Paper cutting applied mathematically.

Hawley, W. M. *Chinese Folk Design.* New York: Dover, 1971.
Illustrations of Chinese paper cuts.

Kuo, Nancy. *Chinese Paper-Cut Pictures.* New York: Taplinger, 1965.
A brief history with illustrations of Chinese paper cuts.

Matisse, Henri. *Jazz.* Munich: H. Piper, ———
Reproduced from the 1947 Paris publication of *Editions Verve* and available through the Museum of Modern Art, New York.

Temko, Florence. *Paper Cutting.* New York: Doubleday, 1973.
A colorful juvenile which is a good introduction for all ages.

Paper sculpture

Sadler, Arthur. *An Introduction to Paper Sculpture.* London: Blandford Press, 1965.

Recording

Kaplan, Dorothy. *Perceptual Development Through Paper Folding.* Deal, New Jersey: Kimbo Educational Records, 1971.
With teacher's manual. For kindergarten through eighth grade.

Film shorts

Creating with Paper, with Florence Temko. Produced by BFA Educational Media, Santa Monica, Calif., 1969.
Origami, with Florence Temko. Produced by National Film Board of Canada, Montreal. World-wide distribution.

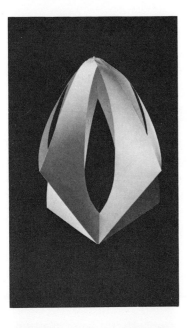

photograph credits

All photographs by Virginia Davidson,
unless stated otherwise.

Joanna Bendheim: Pages 127 (lion), 164 (checkers).
Courtesy, Cepelia Corporation: Pages 112, 113 (lower photo).
Michael Hahn: Pages 14, 17, 19, 26, 32, 36 (deer), 43, 96, 110,
      111, 127 (amatl cut-out), 149, 167 (cone doll).
Carl Kosof: Pages 64 (earrings), 65, 127 (dog).
Courtesy, IBM World Trade Corporation: Pages 38, 39.
Courtesy, The Museum of Contemporary Crafts: Pages 18, 180.
Courtesy, The Origami Center, New York: 34, 35, 41, 84, 187.
Florence Temko: Pages 22, 30, 44, 49 (picture frame), 58, 59,
      113 (upper photo).
Ronald Temko: Pages 125 (YOU cut-out), 168 (first photo).

about the author

Florence Temko is an outstanding authority on paper craft, who is constantly sharing her enthusiasm through classes, lectures and workshops. Her books are an extension of the personal way of teaching which she developed. She was first to realize that paper craft could be presented on television, with the home audience actually participating, as a piece of paper is always handy.

She comes from England and studied at the London School of Economics and later at the New School for Social Research in New York. Her subsequent interest has been in the arts and she has travelled in 28 countries to carry out research on paper craft methods. Her work is shown in museums and schools and she is a consultant to industry. She is the author of PAPERFOLDING TO BEGIN WITH; PAPER CUTTING; FELT CRAFT and other books, and the author of a weekly newspaper column, THINGS TO MAKE. A long time resident of New Jersey, she now lives in Lenox, Massachusetts, where she plans to organize the Paper Craft museum.

about the illustrator

Virginia Davidson, illustrator and assistant designer, studied at the Pratt Institute in New York and is an accomplished artist in sculptural media. Her work has been featured in churches, shopping centers and hospitals, and her varied credits include craft articles in CRAFT HORIZONS and SUNSET MAGAZINE.

about the designer

Joan Stoliar is a graduate of Carnegie Tech. She is now a well known book designer. She designed, as well as illustrated, a previous book by Florence Temko, PAPERFOLDING TO BEGIN WITH. Her other credits include books by Truman Capote, MacKinley Kantor and the best selling JOHNATHAN LIVINGSTON SEAGULL by Richard Bach.